The Smart Craigslist Collection: 3 Books in 1 Volume

How to Have a Side Hustle and Be Successful Selling on Craigslist

Steve Johnson

The Smart Craigslist Guide

How to Buy & Sell and Make Extra Money on Craigslist

Steve Johnson

Copyright © 2019 by Steve Johnson

All Rights Reserved

Disclaimer:

No part of this publication may be reproduced or transmitted in any form or by any means, or transmitted electronically without direct written permission in writing from the author.

While all attempts have been made to verify the information provided in this publication, neither the author nor the publisher assumes any responsibility for errors, omissions, or misuse of the subject matter contained in this eBook.

This eBook is for entertainment purposes only, and the views expressed are those of the author alone, and should not be taken as expert instruction. The reader is responsible for their own actions.

Adherence to applicable laws and regulations, including international, federal, state, and local governing professional licensing business practices, advertising, and all other aspects of doing business in the U.S.A, Canada or any other jurisdiction is the sole responsibility of the purchaser or reader.

Contents

Introduction
    What is Craigslist?
    Navigating Craigslist
Chapter 1: Why Should You Sell on Craigslist?
    Advantages of Using Craigslist to Sell Items
    What Can You Sell on Craigslist?
Chapter 2: Can You Actually Make Money on Craigslist?
    Identify The Item And The Right Price
    Identify Your Niche Interest
    How to Register on Craigslist
Chapter 3: The Correct Way to Sell on Craigslist
    How to Sell Your Item
    Points to Remember When Listing Your Item
Chapter 4: Safety And Meet Ups
    How to Receive Money Safely
    Meet Ups And Collection Tips
Chapter 5: The Smart Way to Buy
    Why Buy From Craigslist?
    Tips For Buying on Craigslist
Chapter 6: How to Avoid Scams
    Questions to Ask Yourself/Things to be Aware of
Chapter 7: How to Get The Most From Craigslist
    Expect Offers, so Price Your Item a Little Higher
    Always Get The Category As Close as Possible
    Focus on Your Headline

> Check Your Contact Information!
>
> Check The Area You're Registered in
>
> Make Your Photographs High Quality
>
> Always Answer Queries

Conclusion

Introduction

> What is Reselling?
>
> How This Book Will Help You

Chapter 1: Why do You Want to be a Reseller on Craigslist?

> The Benefits of Reselling on Craigslist

Chapter 2: What do You Need to Become a Reseller on Craigslist?

Chapter 3: Reselling for Beginners

> Stick to One Item First of All
>
> Also, Stick to One Group of Items
>
> Keep Accurate And Up-To-Date Records
>
> Know Your Rights And The Rights of The Buyer
>
> Safety Comes First
>
> Keep Reality in Your Mind When Looking For Deals
>
> Understand That it Might Take Time

Chapter 4: The Five Important Tasks When Reselling on Craigslist

> Step 1 - Browse Craigslist to Find Deals
>
> Step 2 - Write a Quality Advertisement For Item You're Reselling
>
> Step 3 - Take Quality Photographs
>
> Step 4 - Communicating With The Buyer or Seller
>
> Step 5 - Taking The Item to The Buyer/Picking up The Item

Chapter 5: The Importance of Time Management & Planning

> How to Manage Your Time Effectively
>
> Keep Your Expectations Realistic

Chapter 6: Secrets Tips to Boost Your Selling Power

    Tip 1 - When Selling, Think Like a Buyer

    Tip 2 - Cover All Bases in Your Advertisement

    Tip 3 - Make Sure Your Photos Are High Quality

    Tip 4 - Is The Sale Really Worth it?

    Tip 5 - Give Great Customer Service

    Tip 6 - Build up a Bond of Trust With Your Buyers

Conclusion

Bonus Chapter – Interview with Albert in Vancouver, BC, Canada. Full time reseller on Craigslist

Table of Contents

Introduction

    What This Book is About

    What Does it Take to be a Top Craigslist Seller?

Chapter 1 - The Importance of a Winning Routine

    Why is a Routine Important Generally?

    How to Organize Your Craigslist Reselling Routine Effectively

    Main Points From This Chapter

Chapter 2: Having Fun is The Most Important Thing

    Do Not Allow Reselling to Become a Burden on Your Time

    The Best Mindset For a Craigslist Reseller

    Main Points From This Chapter

Chapter 3: Patience is Key

    Can't Read My Poker Face

    Main Points From This Chapter

Chapter 4: Hedge Your Bets With Several Listings

    Knowing When to Renew Your Listings

    Have a General Meet up Time

- Main Points From This Chapter
- Chapter 5: The Right Way to Negotiate
  - Setting Your Price
  - Expect And Accept The Lowball Attempt
  - Main Points From This Chapter
- Chapter 6: Where to Find Quality Items to Resell
  - What Makes a Good Item, And What Makes a Bad Item?
  - Main Points From This Chapter

Introduction

The Internet is a wonderful thing. We can do our grocery or clothes shopping, search for a vacation, find a job, meet new people, we can even fall in love! Whatever we do these days, we do it online.

There are pros and cons to this constantly switched on way of life, but the Internet is more than an information superhighway, and can actually be used to make cash too.

Yes, by having a strong Internet connection and a little tech-savvy know-how, you can line your bank account either a little or a lot, depending upon your effort level.

You've no doubt heard of eBay. This is an action website which allows you to buy and sell new or used goods for low prices, but have you heard of Craigslist?

Craigslist differs in many different ways to eBay, not least because it's not only about buying and selling old junk, but it's also about advertising services, finding a job, and making cash at the same time. Want to know more? This book is going to give you all the information you need to know on making extra cash on Craigslist, as well as how to avoid the inevitable scams, how to maximize your sales potential, and how to get started from scratch.

First things first, however, you need to know the address!

We are talking about this place - www.craigslist.org

Depending upon where you are in the world, you will be redirected to your local area site and the language spoken in that region. You can change these settings, however, if you prefer to be more international!

What is Craigslist?

Craigslist began from humble seedlings, in San Francisco, and was founded by Craig Newmark and Jim Buckmaster. Craigslist is a classified ads listing site, but the beauty is that you can list quickly and easily, and reach out to countless people in the process. This isn't the same as posting an ad in a local newspaper and hoping someone will read it - in this case, many people will read it!

The site's main job is to act as a host for those advertisements, organizing each is into set categories. Craigslist isn't just about goods to buy and sell, as we mentioned before, it can also be used for services, personal ads, and jobs. The site might look very simple in its design, but this is to allow people to find their way around it much more easily, rather than being dazzled by all singing, all dancing graphics and navigation menus. The simple nature is what makes Craigslist stand out amongst the ad world too.

If you want to enter into the forums, you can do so, and ask questions about items you want to purchase, sell, or anything you're looking for. There is a wealth of information to be found within these forums, and you can be assured of total safety in terms of your identity too.

To give you an idea of how quickly Craigslist has grown, the company began in one city in the USA, and now it covers countless countries and regions across the world, it contains in excess of 25 million classified ads at any one time and more than 1.5 million new postings for jobs. The forums are very active, with around 75 million posts, and it ranks amongst the world's top 10 sites in terms of page views. Basically, if you don't find what you're looking for on Craigslist, you're probably not going to find it at all!

Navigating Craigslist

We already mentioned that Craigslist is a very simple site in terms of its appearance, which is a completely intentional design technique. We are going to go into much more detail in a later chapter about how to actually use Craigslist, but for now, we need to talk about how to find your way around it.

It's a good idea to have your laptop, phone, or tablet close to you whilst reading this book, so you can look at the site at the same time. This will increase your understanding hugely.

If you want to simply look at the site, you can do so without registering, but if you want to actually do anything, e.g. buy something, post a listing, or take part in a forum discussion, you will need to register and sign up to be a member. This is free, and a quick and easy process.

You will see that the listings are organized into categories, and then subcategories. This is designed to make it easier for you to find exactly what you're looking for, rather than scrolling through endless ads for things you have no interest in. For example, you will find a category 'for sale'. If you search within that category you will find subheadings, e.g. furniture, free, garage sale, jewelry, etc. This helps you spend less time searching and more time focused on what you really need.

This book is focused on selling on Craigslist, and therefore making some cold, hard cash from the Internet. You can easily sell the things you no longer want, having a good, old clear out of your garage or home, and decluttering, whilst making cash. It is also worth pointing out and being aware that you can purchase whatever you want from Craigslist, as well as find jobs and services too. Before you read on, have a good, detailed look through the site and browse the various categories. This will give you a basis on which to understand further what we're going to talk about.

Craigslist isn't a difficult site to use, and the mechanics behind it are actually really simple. What you need to be aware of however is a few hidden pieces of information, which will take your sales from 'good', to 'fantastic'. If you know these hints and tips, you'll be able to make more cash than you probably ever realized!

Chapter 1: Why Should You Sell on Craigslist?

Is your home or garage full of junk? Do you have a wardrobe full of clothes that you no longer wear? Are you keen to have an early spring clean and declutter your home?

If you're nodding your head, then you have three main options:

- You can throw it out
- You can donate it to a charity shop
- You can list it on Craigslist and make a profit

The fact you are reading this book tells us that you are firmly in the third option's camp and you want to make some money. Great choice.

In our introduction we talked about what Craigslist is, where it came from, and what you can do with it, but why should you choose Craigslist over other auction and selling sites? eBay is hugely popular and offers a lot of buyer protection, so why should you shun the auction giant and go with Craig instead?

Basically, Craigslist has a few advantages over the other main auction sites online.

Advantages of Using Craigslist to Sell Items

Exactly why should you use Craigslist? Here are a few reasons.

- **No Need to Package and Ship** - If you've ever used eBay in the past, you'll know the euphoria of selling an items quickly diminishes when you have to start packaging up the item, taking it to the post office, having it weighed, shipping it, taking account of shipping costs from what you sold it for, and then praying it gets there in one piece. It's a pain and it takes time and effort. Whilst you factor in the cost of packaging to the price, it doesn't take away the fact that sometimes the shipping price ends up being more, and you lose out. With Craigslist you don't have this issue, because the listing is local. This means you take the item to the person, either by a meet up, or they come to collect from you. We will cover the safety aspects in terms of meet ups in a later chapter, but for now, not having to package up and ship is a major advantage.

- **Easy to Use the Site** - Craigslist is deliberately simple in appearance and in usage. This means anyone can use it, literally anyone. Whilst posting an ad is a little more time consuming than simply searching for something to buy, it is by no means difficult. Once your ad has been posted, you simply sit back and wait for someone to contact you who is interested in purchasing your item. You communicate back and forth, arrange everything and bingo! Sale made!

- **Customer Service Back up** - If you notice you have an issue with a buyer or a seller, you can easily contact customer support for help and advice. Generally speaking, Craigslist staff do not get involved in sales unless there is an issue, but knowing that they're there for you if need be, is a weight off the mind.

- **A Very Convenient Service** - The fact that ads on Craigslist are local means you don't have to deal with time zones and differences, and no misunderstandings in general. The convenience of being able to reach out to a wider number of people means your sale is more likely to be successful too.

- **Your Email Address Isn't Visible** - When you place a posting and communicate with a potential buyer, your email address is kept secret. This takes away the possible worry about privacy issues.

- **It's Free to Place a Listing** - You don't need to pay for your listings, unlike on eBay. There are some anomalies to this point, e.g. if you are posting a job advert, a property advert or a service, but if you're simply selling items, the listing is totally free. This means you can make money on your sales, compared to other auction sites who may take a large percentage cut of the sale.

What Can You Sell on Craigslist?

Basically anything, within reason!

Currently, the sub-categories for sales are:

- Antiques
- Appliances
- Arts & crafts
- Atv/utv/sno
- Auto parts
- Aviation
- Baby & Kid

- Barter
- Beauty & health
- Bike parts
- Bikes
- Boat parts
- Boats
- Books
- Business
- Cars & trucks
- Cds/DVD/VHS
- Cell phones
- Clothes & accessories
- Collectibles
- Computer parts
- Computers
- Electronics
- Farm & garden
- Free
- Furniture
- Garage sale
- General
- Heavy equipment
- Household
- Jewelry
- Materials
- Motorcycle parts
- Motorcycles
- Music instruments
- Photo & Video
- RVS & camping
- Sporting
- Tickets
- Tools
- Toys & Games
- Trailers
- Video gaming
- Wanted
- Wheels & Tires

As you can see, there is plenty of scope in there for whatever you want to sell! This list should give you some idea of the types of things you might have lurking in your house or garage that you could list on Craigslist and potentially make some cash from. If you don't find your category on that list, there is always the 'general' sub-category, but do be aware that the more specific you can be in terms of which category you list your item in, the greater the chance of making a sale.

For most people, the answer to 'why sell your items on Craigslist' is about decluttering and cash. Those are two fantastic reasons to go with but remember that you can use Craigslist to find a job, access services, and speak to people on the forums too. The more sales you make, the more you are likely to use Craigslist for your other endeavors too. Familiarizing yourself with the site, working slowly, and listing one thing at a time for the first few times you use it, will help you to streamline your selling and avoid any potential pitfalls.

Whilst Craigslist is very easy to use, a sale isn't definite until you have traded cash for the item, and in-between that time, communication breakdowns and issues can easily derail your profit-making efforts!

Chapter 2: Can You Actually Make Money on Craigslist?

The reason we are writing this book is simply that the answer to that question is a very large 'yes'!

At first, you cannot expect to get rich from Craigslist, but that really does depend on what you have to sell and how you sell it. You should begin by having a clear out and selling the things you do not need anymore. There is no use in hoarding items if you don't use them - if that item hasn't seen the light of day for the last year and it has no sentimental value to you, get it listed!

There are two ways you can make cash from Craigslist:

- Selling items you already have, which you no longer need
- Reselling in-demand items for a profit

Later on in the book, we are going to talk about hints and tips to maximize sales, and we're also going to talk about how to list an item properly, but for now, these are the things you need to know which could affect how much cash you make from your Craigslist sales.

Selling the items you have in your house which you no longer need is the quickest and easiest way to make money from the site, but as you become more familiar with it, and the more you successfully sell, you might like to take a step further. There are many professional sellers on sites like Amazon and eBay, and you can do the same with Craigslist if you put in the time and effort to find the items which are in demand, which sell for a good price, and which are easy to source.

For instance, you could go into the cell phone case business (a very in-demand area, but just as an example). This means you would look at how much cell phone cases were selling for and how much they cost to buy, check if there is a real saturation of the market in your area or whether there is space for you too, and then purchase some in, or buy when you need, and sell on for a greater profit. You could easily use this as a passive income method!

So, where to start?

Identify The Item And The Right Price

It's a good idea to identify the item you want to sell and then head online and do some research on how much it would cost to buy it new. Obviously, if you're selling things you already have in your home, you shouldn't try and sell the item for the brand-new price, because your item is second hand and therefore the cost needs to be lower. What you can do is use other auction sites and find similar items, and see how much they are selling for there. This gives you a good guideline on how much to ask for, and will avoid overcharging, or even worse, losing out on money yourself by undercharging!

If the item has any defects, e.g. any chips, breakages, or anything else cosmetically or mechanically wrong with it, you will need to list this, and the price will need to be lower to reflect this defect. This is something to bear in mind. Never list something as being in perfect condition if it isn't. You will be caught out and your sale will not go ahead. Be honest at all times. Look at it this way, you wouldn't want the same to happen to you, would you?

Identify Your Niche Interest

If you really want to go down the line of selling on Craigslist on a regular basis, you need to identify the niche you're going to work with. It's no good jumping from one area to another, as you're simply going to confuse yourself, and you cannot become an expert in every single selling area! It's best to specialize in one or two niches, e.g. the cell phone case example we just mentioned, and you could then branch out into laptop cases in the future.

By understanding how in demand your niche is and the prices you can expect to buy and sell for, you can see whether or not you have chosen the right area, or whether you would be better to switch areas and find greater profits elsewhere. Making money from Craigslist might not happen overnight, so do be prepared to learn about the niche you want to specialize in properly and understand how to price each item realistically. When you communicate with customers, they want to know that they are dealing with someone who is genuine and who understands what they are trying to sell. This will reduce the chances of a sale falling through.

How to Register on Craigslist

Once you've decided you want to go ahead and sell items on Craigslist, you will need to register for a free account. This enables you to sell items, buy items, and use the forums. Registering is free, very quick, and very easy.

When registering you simply click 'my account' on the main page. This will then take you to a page which asks for your log in details, or it will ask you to 'create account'. In order to create your account, you simply need to enter your email address. Once you have done this will you be sent a verification email, which you simply need to click to verify you are indeed who you say you are!

That's it! You are now registered to buy, sell, and use the forums on Craigslist.

You can post your item for free, and you do not pay any fees if you sell it. That's the major upside of Craigslist, compared to other auction sites, such as eBay. Do be aware, however, if you want to post a job listing, a property listing, or you want to post about a service, you will need to pay fees, but for the purposes of this book we are talking about selling items, so those fees shouldn't really apply to you.

Chapter 3: The Correct Way to Sell on Craigslist

Now you've decided that you want to use Craigslist to make some cash, it's time to find out exactly how to go about selling things correctly, in order to ensure success comes your way. Again, a little later we're going to dedicate a whole chapter to tips on maximizing your sales, but in this chapter, we will take about the main areas to bear in mind, in order to make your first sale.

Remember to go ahead and register for your free account before you even start trying to work towards selling anything on Craigslist. It is quick, easy, and free, and as soon as you're set up, you're good to go. This also gives you access to the forums which are a great source of information within the site. You can go on here and read threads, and if you want to take part in a conversation you can; if you just want to read and soak up some knowledge, you can do that too!

Let's go through a step by step guide on how to make sure you sell your item, or items, correctly on Craigslist.

How to Sell Your Item

Identify Your Item And Make Sure it is Suitable

We talked in our last chapter about finding things within your home or garage which you don't want anymore, and this is the ideal place to start. What you need to find out however is whether the item you want to sell is suitable. Does it work? Are there too many cosmetic defects with it? If so, it's not the best idea to try and sell it and your effort will be wasted. If however, there is nothing wrong with it mechanically, or to a degree, and it looks great, you can go ahead and list it.

Remember to look through the categories we talked about in our last chapter. If you identify the right category, as close to your item as possible, then you have more chance of a sale. The reason for this is because when someone is searching for a particular item to buy, they will be as direct as possible. This means they will look in the category which makes the most sense, and if it's not there, they're not likely to go searching through loose-fitting categories. It's a little like the search results you see on Google - most people only look at the first page, the second page if they're lucky, but they do not really go beyond that. Category choosing is the same kind of process, so make sure you're as specific as you can possibly be. If you're not too sure, spend some time browsing, to get a clearer idea of where the item should go.

For instance, a gel nail lamp would go under beauty and health, a car engine would go under car parts, etc.

Choosing The Correct Price

Now you know what you want to sell and you know which category fits it best, you need to come up with a fair price. This price needs to be attractive enough to gain attention and make people want to buy your product, but it also needs to be high enough to make the sale worth your time. If you go too low, you're sure to sell your item quite probably, but you'll lose out on its worth. If you go too high, nobody is going to think your item is worth buying, because they can probably go out and buy a new version for the same, or very similar. It's a fine line to walk!

The best advice, as before, is to do some research online into how much the item retails for when new, and then look online at other auction sites to see how much it sells for second hand. Come to a good piece of middle ground, which not only covers your profit but also doesn't take the price too far away from being attractive to the buyer. Research is key in this regard and will be the difference between a sale, and no cash coming your way at all.

Take Quality Photographs

If you list your item without a photograph it is extremely unlikely to sell. For that reason, you need to take a very good photo of the item you're selling and you also need to photograph any defects that are part of the sale. These need to be added to the description, but a visual is always better for helping the buyer to understand just how bad/minimal the defect is.

Hopefully there will be no defect and in that case, you can simply go ahead and photograph the item in the best possible light, without any distractions in the background. The more professional your photo looks, this will increase the chances of the buyer trusting you as a seller. Obviously, make sure the item is clean and in the best possible state as you take a photo of it!

The more photos you can include in your listing, the better. Most people tend to buy items which have more than one photo, but at the very least make sure you have one very high-quality photo of the item. If you are going to add in more than one image, you should take photos from different sides, so the buyer has plenty of information on the visual side of the item you're trying to sell.

Create a Clear Headline

The headline is basically the name of the item you're trying to sell, so don't be too obscure and be as direct and clear as possible. If you are selling a gel nail lamp, call it a gel nail lamp, and don't go too far into specifics, e.g. a UV thermal nail heating machine! Stick to basics, as that is what people will search for when they browse the site for the items they want to buy the most.

By making your item easy to be searched for, it will appear in search results much more often, and as a result, you are much more likely to make a sale. The specifics of the item will then be outlined in the description, which we'll come onto shortly. If the item is sub-standard, e.g. part of it doesn't work, it's up to you whether you highlight this in the headline, or whether you leave that until the description. This is a grey area in many ways because if the reader sees anything about it not working in tip-top condition, they're probably going to flick over to the next item. If however, you catch their attention with the first headline and then give them the information in more detail in the description, they may still be inclined to buy it. For that reason, perhaps leave it until the description.

Write a Clear And Helpful Description

This is where you get to sell your item in the best possible light. The description shouldn't be too long, as you don't want to bore potential buyers, but it needs to give them all the information they need. For that reason, consider using bullet points to outline the features of the product. The description should contain:

- The name and brand of the item
- The age of the item
- The working order, e.g. if there is any defect, and the details if so
- Any accessories included with the product
- Is it in the original packaging/box?
- Any item specifics which you feel are necessary, but keep this brief
- Features, in a bullet point list (if necessary)

The description shouldn't be too sales-like, and instead should be clear and polite. Also, make sure that the format of your description is easy to read, and that the potential buyer can skim read the main details if necessary, rather than having large paragraph blocks of text. This is another reason why bullet points work well.

Decide How You Want People to Contact You

You can leave either your email, your telephone number, or you can enter both. It is best to include your phone number because that way you are more likely to make a sale. The reason is that people still like to pick up the phone and call quickly; they think if they do this, they are going to get in there before anyone else, as their email could be lost within your inbox quite easily. If you don't want to leave your phone number, that's also fine, but be aware that you might make potential buyers contacting you slightly less likely.

If you are only going to leave your email, make sure you check your inbox on a regular basis, so you don't keep people waiting for replies.

Sell Your Item!

From there, you're ready to submit your item and wait for buyers to start messaging or calling you. It might take a while, it might be instant, so it's important to be patient and not to become obsessed with checking every five minutes! Having said that, keep your inbox within sight, as we mentioned before.

Clean Your Item and Box it

It's a good idea, whilst you're waiting for buyers to contact you, to clean up the item and box it up, ready for collection. You do not have to package your item in the same way you would if you were selling your item on eBay, but you do want to make it easy for the person to carry the item away from your ownership, e.g. in a box or a large bag. Make sure you clean your item well, ready for the sale to be completed.

Points to Remember When Listing Your Item

Listing an item for sale on Craigslist is quite easy, and provided you have all the information to hand, it shouldn't take you too long. If you need more information on the features of the product, you can always research this online and use the details you find. The most important thing to remember is to always be honest and not to stretch the truth when it comes to the quality of your item or any of the features.

If you want to avoid problems after the sale has gone through, you need to make sure that you tell the truth. Look at it this way - would you want to buy something, pay money, get it home and then realize that it isn't what you were promised at all? Of course not! In this case, always be honest with the listing details and if there are any problems or defects with it, it's best to speak up at this point, then deal with the issues later on. A product which has a few cosmetic issues or a defect isn't necessarily going to not sell, and it's often the case that people are happy to accept a slightly sub-standard product, as long as the price reflects that.

Also make sure that your description is easy to scan, easy to read, and has the right friendly and polite tone. You are not a store trying to sell something online, so avoid overly sales-focused language.

Overall, be aware of the following points:

- Be honest and open about the product
- Make your description easy to read

- Don't make the description too long
- Don't overprice or underprice the product
- Check your contact details before listing the product
- Clean the product well, in anticipation of the sale

Once you are contacted by a potential buyer, make sure you answer in a timely manner, to avoid them becoming tired of waiting, and therefore you miss out on the cash!

Chapter 4: Safety And Meet Ups

You've made a sale, congratulations!

The next thing you need to do is arrange to meet up to pass the item over or have the item collected from you. Of course, as with any type of meeting someone you don't know endeavor, you need to exercise caution and common sense. Do not simply give someone your home address and ask them to come over when you're home alone. You do not know this person. Whilst we would hope that they are perfectly fine and honest, you simply shouldn't take the risk.

We should point out that the overwhelming majority of sales on Craigslist are conducted completely professionally and there are rarely any problems, but your safety is not something you should gamble with, so a few precautions and safeguards should be put in place.

How to Receive Money Safely

When making a sale on Craigslist, you have two options in terms of being paid:

- In cash
- Via PayPal

The single best way to receive the money from your Craigslist sale is by cash when the person collects the item. You could use PayPal also, and we'll cover that in a second. Never give someone your bank details and ask them to deposit the money. You might think this is quicker and easier, but giving someone your personal bank details is risky, and you do not know who you are dealing with!

Of course, you should not give the item to anyone without receiving the cash at the same time. For this reason, meetups or collections should always be along the lines of 'here is the money', and then 'here is the item'.

This is also something you should point out to the buyer when you are speaking to them before the sale is finalized. This cuts down on any confusion and ensures that the sale goes through much quicker and easier than otherwise.

Should you accept payment by PayPal? This is another possibility, because it is usually linked to your home email address, and the banking side of things is anonymous. If the amount of cash is large, or the person simply doesn't want to draw out the cash and bring it to you, you could ask them to deposit the correct amount prior to you giving them the item, and that gives you time to check the money goes through properly. If there are any delays with the deposit being made, e.g. the funds are held before crediting to your account, wait to give them the item until the delay is cleared up.

How you are going to receive the money is something you should talk about with the buyer when you are communicating back and forth, and it is important to be clear on arrangements from the start. Never accept payment from anyone who makes it difficult, e.g if they are asking for bank details and not willing to deviate from their wishes, or they are asking if payment can be made from a source which you simply don't feel right about.

There are some strange people out there! That's not to say you're going to meet one, but it's important to be careful in terms of checking that you actually receive the money, before you hand over the item. Remember, you can always try and sell again, but if you hand it over and don't get paid, you're completely out of pocket.

Meet Ups And Collection Tips

The fact you are meeting someone you do not know means you need to exercise caution, and this means using your common sense above everything else. Of course, not everyone you sell items to on Craigslist is going to threaten your safety, but it pays to always be on your guard!

How you pass the item to the buyer depends on a few things, mainly on whether or not you drive, and how badly you actually want to make the sale. If you drive, life gets a little easier, as that means you can arrange a mutually convenient point to make the sale, i.e. in public. If you don't drive, that means you're going to have to use public transport to get to your meeting point, which could be time-consuming and it's also going to cost you money in terms of bus/train fares. The point you meet at has to be convenient for you both, but possibly more so for you because this shouldn't be costing you any money!

Here are a few tips for arranging meetups and collections for items you sell on Craigslist.

Never Arrange Collections From Home

Your safety is vital, so never arrange for the item to be collected from your home, or from someone else's home. Giving your address out is not a good idea, and you don't know who is going to be turning up at your door. They may not even be alone. In this case, arranging a meeting point is always a better option. If the buyer presses to collect the item from your home because it's quicker, explain that you are often out, at work, etc, and make your excuses. If they still won't budge from their request, it's best to try and sell to someone else. Yes, you might miss out on the sale, but what is their reason for being so adamant on visiting your house? That is something you have to ask yourself.

Always Meet in Public

Choose a meeting point which is in a public space, e.g. a shopping mall, a coffee shop, or a restaurant. Never arrange to meet up in a car park or somewhere which is a relatively desolate area. Keep in mind that you need people milling around you in order to create a sense of safety for you. Of course, meeting in public is also a matter of safety for the buyer too, as whilst we're focusing on the fact that you don't know them, they don't know you either! Keeping the process in the public eye will protect you both and make you both feel easier and assured about the sale going through to completion successfully.

Day Time is Better

Meeting in the daytime is always better than meeting at night or when the night is falling. Again, this is a matter of safety and being seen in public, and it also makes the meeting process easier because you can see each other! If you meet in the dark, you can easily miss one another and this is going to make the delivery process harder.

Mid-afternoon or mid-mornings are good times to meet, as they're convenient for most people and these are also busy times in public places. If the weather is particularly bad, e.g. very heavy rain which is making visibility difficult or making the day seem strangely dark, rearrange the collection and meet another time. Not only will your buyer probably not want to head out in the rain, but dark conditions are simply not safe for you either.

Be Flexible in Order to Confirm Safety

It's important to come to a mutually convenient time and place for both of you, but there may be times when this is difficult, e.g. due to work or family commitments. The best advice is to do your very best in terms of making the collection process as quick and easy as possible. It isn't going to take more than five minutes maximum for the handing over of the cash and the item, so if it is possible to quickly head out of work on a break, you could do that. It's always best to put yourself out in terms of rushing a little, rather than trying to meet someone in a time which is deemed unsafe. Safety has to come first, and this is something which should come over and above your eagerness to make a sale.

Chapter 5: The Smart Way to Buy

We've talked so far about selling items on Craigslist and making cash from it, but if we flip the coin to the opposite side, it's entirely possible to save money by buying on Craigslist too! There are some real bargains to be found, and if you're looking for something obscure or something you're struggling to find in stores, you might very well find someone having a clear out and selling the item you've been looking for.

As with selling, there are a few things you need to bear in mind, and a few safety considerations to think about too. Familiarizing yourself with the site and how it all works before you start to buy anything is vital. You might have been looking at the site from a seller's point of view to date, but buying is a slightly different area. Being aware of the site from all angles will help you to avoid any pitfalls, and find the biggest bargains around.

Why Buy From Craigslist?

We've talked in detail throughout the book to date about why you should sell your unwanted items on Craigslist, and why you should even think about purchasing goods to resell on, but what about buying - why should you purchase items from Craigslist?

Everyone out there has been doing the same as you to date - they have been having household clear outs and they're trying to sell the things they no longer want for a little extra cash. There is nothing particularly worrying or offhand about that, and provided you do your research into what you're buying, you could find yourself with a serious bargain in your midst.

The main advantages of buying from Craigslist are:

- You can find items for sale which are probably not in the shops
- You can arrange your price to a certain degree, so you save cash and grab some bargains
- You are able to browse the site when it suits you, so your purchases are convenient
- Sales are done locally, so you don't have to worry about shipping and possible delays
- You can ask questions about the item and make sure it is really what you're looking for

Let's take antiques, for example. Whilst there are many antique dealers out there, finding the one pieces you've been searching years for can be a case of luck. Someone has found an item in their garage and they have no clue what it is. It was handed down to them by a member of the distant family and they simply want to get rid of it because it's cluttering the place up and collecting dust. That item is the piece you've been searching for and because the buyer doesn't really have a lot of antique knowledge, you can purchase it for a lower price than if you went to an expert dealer.

Most people on Craigslist aren't trying to make the world's biggest profit, they're simply trying to sell their items for a fair price. This means great items for you, at low prices.

Tips For Buying on Craigslist

Don't Just Buy For The Sake of It

It's very easy to sit at home with your laptop, browsing shopping sites, and thinking 'oh, I'll buy that!' What you need to do is ask yourself if you really need it. If you do, go for it; if you're simply making impulse buys, it's probably going to end up back on Craigslist at a later date, when you have a household clear out too!

Only purchase items that you are very sure you want, and be prepared to go through the process of contacting the buyer, arranging the collection, and actually going to pick up the item and hand over the cash. Don't be a time waster, and don't be someone who purchases for the sake of it and then wishes they didn't!

Is it a Good Deal or Not?

It really depends on what you're buying, but is the item really that good of a deal? This is where you need to do some research into prices and specifics before you make contact with the buyer and express an interest. The reason many people bypass this stage is that they're so keen to get in there first and not miss out on purchasing the item, that they rush trying to find out what they're getting themselves into. Don't worry about missing out - if you're supposed to get it, you will, and it's always better to give yourself an extra half an hour of research time than end up buying an item for much more than its worth in the end.

Head online and look at other auction sites, to discover how much the same item is being sold for elsewhere. Also look at the cost of buying the item brand new, and work out whether or not the asking price is fair, or even low enough to consider snapping their hand off.

Negotiate But Don't Lowball Someone

It is entirely possible and probably expected that you try and negotiate the price. If you're selling an item, this is going to happen to you, and it's always better to try and work with the buyer than simply say 'no'. If they are asking for a ridiculously low price, of course, you are well within your rights to refuse, but it's a good idea to consider other offers.

When you find an item you want to buy and you've done your research into how much it should cost, message the seller and offer a slightly lower price. Do not lowball a seller, it's just not good sense. You wouldn't want someone to do the same thing to you, and quite frankly it's insulting. Whatever price you try and negotiate to, make sure it is fair for both of you. If your new offer is accepted, great, you've got yourself a bargain. If not, consider paying the asking price, or moving on.

Always be Polite

This goes without saying, but always be polite with a seller. You're more likely to clinch the sale if you're polite with them, rather than being someone who is asking far too many unnecessary questions, over-messaging, and offering insulting prices. Always put yourself in the shoes of the seller and consider their feelings at the same time. Remember, people selling on Craigslist are not in serious business, they are just people trying to sell their items and make a little cash!

Why Are They Selling?

If the item is being sold for a great price and the product is in fantastic condition, you really need to ask the question of why they are selling it in the first place. It's not rude to ask this question, and any seller should be prepared to hear it and answer it. It is quite likely that they're selling it because they simply don't need it anymore and it's taking up precious space in their house or garage. That's a fine and very viable excuse. On the other hand, the answer could set alarm bells in your mind, and that is when you probably need to take our next step and ask whether or not you can test out the item before parting with any cash.

Someone who seems overly-eager to sell an item for a low price, despite listing it as in tip-top condition with no mechanical issues, could be being a little less than honest about the item's condition.

Can You Try The Item Before You Buy it?

If you are parting with a large amount of cash, or the item is mechanical or very large, then you can ask if you can try the item out first. For instance, many people sell cars on Craigslist, and you're not going to hand over cash without looking it over in person first! The same goes for anything electronic - you need to know that it is working correctly before you commit 100% to buy it. If a seller says 'no' then you need to really be a little suspicious and ask yourself why.

An honest and open seller should have no problem with you trying the item out, and will help to make arrangements for that to happen. They might not want you to go to their house to test it out, and that's something you need to respect because it's about their safety, but they should make other arrangements instead.

Take Someone With You

If you are buying something large and you simply cannot meet in public, then always take someone with you when you go to collect or try out the product. Do not go alone as you have no idea where you are going, and who is going to be waiting for you when you arrive. Taking a trusted friend or family member with you, and letting someone else know where you are going, and the details of the address, is simply good safety sense, and something any self-respecting seller should expect you to be doing also. If the seller doesn't want you to go with another person, steer clear and cancel the sale. Alarm bells should ring in that case.

Buying items on Craigslist is a great way to find bargains, large items, and rare items. Provided you ask the right questions and check everything out before handing over the cash, you could find yourself with the item you've always wanted. Of course, buying items also gives you the opportunity to sell them on for a greater profit, so always be on the lookout for fantastic bargains too.

Chapter 6: How to Avoid Scams

We've talked a lot so far in this book not only about how to use Craigslist but also about safety. This isn't an accident - whilst Craigslist itself is a very safe site, the fact you are meeting up with and communicating with people you have never met before means you need to keep your guard up. This advice is certainly not only apparent with Craigslist, but with any buying and selling site which involves you meeting other people.

In addition to that, you need to careful about possible scams.

Wherever there are people, there are always going to be a mix of good and bad. This is something no site can stop from happening, and all you can do is be extra careful. We should point out that the huge majority of transactions on Craigslist are completely above board, legit, and very honest. The people who speak on forums are also 99% honest, open, and friendly, but there is always bound to be a very small minority who are out to ruin it for the rest.

Don't let them win, simply keep your wits about you and be educated on the possible scams that might be lurking out there.

Questions to Ask Yourself/Things to be Aware of

Is This Deal Too Good to be True?

It pays to be a little suspicious sometimes, and if you notice someone is selling a quality product for a rather low price, you need to ask yourself why. We have touched upon this already, but sometimes a seller is trying to offload a defect product for a better price, without giving you the real low down on the quality or status of the product.

You can easily get around this possible scam by asking the seller why they are actually selling the item. Their answer should tell you quite a lot, and you can also ask directly if there are any defects in the product. We're going to talk shortly about the tone of voice and language used but never distrust your gut. If you're asking these direct questions and they are hesitating or being overly defensive, there is probably something they're not telling you. Again, you can ask to try the product before you buy it also, but never go alone and always take someone else with you.

Listen to Your Gut

Do you trust the person and what they are telling you? Have a phone conversation with them and listen to their tone of voice. Whilst it's possible that the person is just shy and not great at speaking to strangers over the phone, there are some tell-tale signs which point towards rather shifty behavior. Signs to look out for include:

- Saying 'umm', 'ahh', 'err' a lot when you are asking direct questions they should know the answer to
- What is their tone of voice like? Are they speaking very fast? Do they sound nervous? These are signs that something might not be as it seems
- They are very vague on details. A person selling an item should know about what they're selling and should be able to answer all necessary questions
- They refuse to compromise on anything

At the end of the day, your gut will not let you down and if you're simply getting a feeling that something isn't quite right, it's best to pass on the sale and look for someone who is a little more upfront and honest. If you are the one doing the selling and it is a buyer who you're not quite sure about, there is nothing wrong with possibly telling the person that the item is no longer available. It is better to tell a little white lie and get yourself out of the situation than be forced to meet someone who you really aren't quite sure about. Again, safety is key.

Do They Give Their Telephone Number?

A scammer, whether a buyer or a seller, will not give you their telephone number and will insist only on email contact. It might also be the case that they don't want to be contacted via the regular email they have used to register for Craigslist, and they will ask you to message them via a different address, which is likely to look a little odd. This is because messages cannot be reached from the Craigslist point of view, once the communication is out of their registered address.

It is normal for some people not to want to give out their telephone number to people they don't know, and that is why this one is quite hard to manage. What you should do however is listen to what your gut says, and if that is screaming 'scam!', then you should listen.

Do They Ask For Other Payment Methods?

For your own safety and security only ever ask for cash or PayPal when buying or selling. Cash is always preferable, but there may be times when that is not possible. In that case, make sure the PayPal transaction has gone through and is registered on the transaction history as coming from the person making the purchase or sale before you hand over the item.

If the person is constantly asking for your bank details because they can't do it any other way, they don't have PayPal, or some other reason which you simply don't feel easy about, do not listen. Do not give your bank details out to anyone, especially someone you meet via a purchase or sale on Craigslist.

Avoid Buying or Selling Expensive Items at First

When you first start using Craigslist, it is best to start slow and low. Avoid making large cash sales or purchases until you have a little more Craigslist experience. There are some people out there who will take advantage of someone who seems to be inexperienced in using the site, and whilst you can fake confidence, these people are quite clever and know the signs to look for. Stick with low priced products at first and as your confidence and experience grow, you can use the site for larger and higher priced purchases.

Always Test Out Electronics

Electronics are probably the number on scam area, because these can be purchased from anywhere in the world, and could also be extremely fake. Unless you see it for yourself and test it out, you could be buying extremely substandard equipment and paying well over the odds for it. If they refuse to let you test it, shrug your shoulders and move on, because that is a sure fire sign of a scam.

The best advice when it comes to using Craigslist for the first few times is to simply be aware that there are scams out there and to be very careful. You will become more used to the things that are asked of you naturally, and the questions to put to a seller, but when you are new it's important to start slowly. Being suspicious of everyone might sound like a rather negative mindset, but it's best to be protective of yourself and your cash with people you just don't know.

Chapter 7: How to Get The Most From Craigslist

By this point in the book, you should be quite sure that there is a very real possibility to make cash from selling and reselling on Craigslist. What you need to know now, is how to maximize those sales and give yourself the very best chance of lining your bank account.

We have already touched upon some of the best tips already as we've moved through the various topics we have covered, but to give you a quick reference guide, here are some of the very best hints and tips to help you get the most from your sales on Craigslist.

Expect Offers, so Price Your Item a Little Higher

You might think this is contradictory because we've talked about giving prices which are in line with what else is offered online, but that doesn't mean that you can't be savvy and price your item around 2-3% higher. The reason is that buyers are likely to contact you and try and negotiate the price. If you put the price as what you've researched online, and then you negotiate with a prospective buyer, you're going to miss out. By placing the price around 3% higher maximum, you're giving yourself wiggle room, and you won't end up with a loss of profits.

Always Get The Category As Close as Possible

We have covered this one already but it is so vitally important we need to mention it again. When listing an item for sale, you need to choose the most accurate category possible. People do not eat to spend endless hours searching through every item for sale on the entirety of Craigslist in their region, so make life a little easier for them. If you're not sure, then do some more research, but the closest match you choose, the more likely it is that someone is going to find your item and contact you about buying it.

Focus on Your Headline

In terms of grabbing attention, your headline is the thing you need to focus on. By being as clear and simple as possible, you will attract more possible buyers your way. If you're too intricate and you use language which only an expert in that particular item would know, you're cutting out your chances of working with less than experts, or newbies to Craigslist. Stick to basics.

Check Your Contact Information!

Do you know how many people have listed an item on Craigslist and then wondered why nobody is contacting them? It's because they put the wrong phone number down, or they missed out a number in their email address! The most simple thing in the world, but double check your contact information before you list the item for sale and you will enhance your chances by a million!

Check The Area You're Registered in

Check that you are listing your item in the correct region. For instance, if you live in New York, make sure you are selling the item with the borough or few boroughs closest to your home. Unless you want to travel all the way across the New York state, this will eliminate the chances of selling an item, only for it to fall through when it comes to arranging collection.

Make Your Photographs High Quality

It's no good taking a blurry photograph of the item with your phone and expecting interest to come your way. The photos you take need to be high quality and they need to show all sides of the item. For that reason, consider posting more than one photo, especially if there are any defects or cosmetic issues.

Always Answer Queries

Surely this is obvious, but you should always answer questions which come your way via email or telephone. This person could be your new buyer, but if you're too busy to answer their email, or you just don't want to answer the phone right at that moment and forget to call back, you could miss the sale entirely. There is nothing to say that someone else is going to contact you instead, so always make sure you return calls and reply to emails. It's just polite if nothing else!

By knowing the tricks of the trade and being as open and honest as possible, you can easily maximize your potential Craigslist sales and make a tidy profit.

Conclusion

And there we have it! Your complete guide to making cash from Craigslist, either by clearing out your garage and selling on the items you no longer use, or actually buying items and reselling them for a profit. Whichever route you go down, having the expert knowledge on how to actually go about it will stand you in great stead.

Having a house or garage clear out is the ideal way to get started on Craigslist, but as your confidence grows, you could easily branch out into reselling. As we have mentioned, this means purchasing items and then selling them on for a profit. There are certain niches which are more popular than others for reselling, and the main ones are books, cellphones, cellphone accessories, and computer parts or hardware. These are the types of items which are often searched for on local selling sites, rather than purchasing them on large auction sites or new from online brands. You can usually find great bargains in this way, which is why most people will use sites such as Craigslist first and foremost.

Of course, that's not to say that you can't look at other niches, but it's vital to do your research beforehand. Take some time looking at the types of products which are already for sale and see how quickly they remain there, and how quickly the posting is taken down. Once the posting has gone, the item has been sold. This should tell you a lot about how popular those products are. If you notice the same item or a similar one is up for sale a day or so later, this person is reselling, and that niche is therefore quite in demand.

Overall, the most important points to take away from this book are:

- Craigslist is a local classified ads site, which allows you to buy and sell from people within your local area
- Listing an item for sale is completely free, however, you will pay a small amount if you are listing for a property, a job, or certain services, e.g. holistic
- Once you sell the item, you do not pay any fees, which makes Craigslist preferable to large sites, such as eBay
- You do not need to package or post items to buyers, as the collection is done via a meetup
- Safety is vital when it comes to meeting a buyer or a seller, and you should always exercise caution and common sense, e.g. never go to someone's house or have anyone come to your house
- There are certain scams which might take place on Craigslist, and knowing about these ahead of time, and using your gut, will help you to avoid any unfortunate circumstances
- Always be honest when selling items on Craigslist
- Always list your item in the right category, to avoid missing a sale because the product was too hard to find. Remember, there are countless products

for sale on Craigslist within any specific area, and nobody wants to look through all of them!
- When setting the price you want to sell a product for, always go around 2-3% higher, as the buyer is likely to try and negotiate the price with you anyway
- Ensure you take high-quality photographs of items as you post them, and if possible, post more than one photo to enhance the chances of a sale
- Never give out your bank details or any other financial information to a buyer or a seller. Only ever use cash, and if that isn't possible, PayPal as a last resort

These are the main points you should be more than aware of by this point in the book. Remember to start slow and keep your sales and purchases low cost as you begin your journey into making cash from Craigslist. As your experience and confidence grow, you can quickly increase your profit margin, but working slowly will allow you to gain the necessary knowledge and avoid any potential pitfalls that might otherwise come your way.

All that is left to say is 'good luck'!

THE ADVANCED CRAIGSLIST RESELLER GUIDE

How to Make Extra Money or Create a Side Income By Reselling On Craigslist

Steve Johnson

Contents

Introduction
    What is Craigslist?
    Navigating Craigslist

Chapter 1: Why Should You Sell on Craigslist?
    Advantages of Using Craigslist to Sell Items
    What Can You Sell on Craigslist?

Chapter 2: Can You Actually Make Money on Craigslist?
    Identify The Item And The Right Price
    Identify Your Niche Interest
    How to Register on Craigslist

Chapter 3: The Correct Way to Sell on Craigslist
    How to Sell Your Item
    Points to Remember When Listing Your Item

Chapter 4: Safety And Meet Ups
    How to Receive Money Safely
    Meet Ups And Collection Tips

Chapter 5: The Smart Way to Buy
    Why Buy From Craigslist?
    Tips For Buying on Craigslist

Chapter 6: How to Avoid Scams
    Questions to Ask Yourself/Things to be Aware of

Chapter 7: How to Get The Most From Craigslist
    Expect Offers, so Price Your Item a Little Higher
    Always Get The Category As Close as Possible
    Focus on Your Headline
    Check Your Contact Information!
    Check The Area You're Registered in

- Make Your Photographs High Quality
- Always Answer Queries

Conclusion

Introduction
- What is Reselling?
- How This Book Will Help You

Chapter 1: Why do You Want to be a Reseller on Craigslist?
- The Benefits of Reselling on Craigslist

Chapter 2: What do You Need to Become a Reseller on Craigslist?

Chapter 3: Reselling for Beginners
- Stick to One Item First of All
- Also, Stick to One Group of Items
- Keep Accurate And Up-To-Date Records
- Know Your Rights And The Rights of The Buyer
- Safety Comes First
- Keep Reality in Your Mind When Looking For Deals
- Understand That it Might Take Time

Chapter 4: The Five Important Tasks When Reselling on Craigslist
- Step 1 - Browse Craigslist to Find Deals
- Step 2 - Write a Quality Advertisement For Item You're Reselling
- Step 3 - Take Quality Photographs
- Step 4 - Communicating With The Buyer or Seller
- Step 5 - Taking The Item to The Buyer/Picking up The Item

Chapter 5: The Importance of Time Management & Planning
- How to Manage Your Time Effectively
- Keep Your Expectations Realistic

Chapter 6: Secrets Tips to Boost Your Selling Power
- Tip 1 - When Selling, Think Like a Buyer

Tip 2 - Cover All Bases in Your Advertisement

Tip 3 - Make Sure Your Photos Are High Quality

Tip 4 - Is The Sale Really Worth it?

Tip 5 - Give Great Customer Service

Tip 6 - Build up a Bond of Trust With Your Buyers

Conclusion

Bonus Chapter – Interview with Albert in Vancouver, BC, Canada. Full time reseller on Craigslist

Table of Contents

Introduction

What This Book is About

What Does it Take to be a Top Craigslist Seller?

Chapter 1 - The Importance of a Winning Routine

Why is a Routine Important Generally?

How to Organize Your Craigslist Reselling Routine Effectively

Main Points From This Chapter

Chapter 2: Having Fun is The Most Important Thing

Do Not Allow Reselling to Become a Burden on Your Time

The Best Mindset For a Craigslist Reseller

Main Points From This Chapter

Chapter 3: Patience is Key

Can't Read My Poker Face

Main Points From This Chapter

Chapter 4: Hedge Your Bets With Several Listings

Knowing When to Renew Your Listings

Have a General Meet up Time

Main Points From This Chapter

Chapter 5: The Right Way to Negotiate

- Setting Your Price
- Expect And Accept The Lowball Attempt
- Main Points From This Chapter
- Chapter 6: Where to Find Quality Items to Resell
  - What Makes a Good Item, And What Makes a Bad Item?
  - Main Points From This Chapter

Introduction

These days, there are many ways in which to make a profit if you look hard enough. Some of these avenues might not seem obvious at first, but once you do your research and think a little outside of the box, you'll be surprised at some of the ways you can make cash for whatever endeavor you're focusing on.

The bottom line is that life can be expensive, and with increasing prices and static wages, more and more people are choosing to find sidelines to make extra cash. This can be a substantial amount, or perhaps just a little extra cash and here and there. Regardless of the amount, having a profitable sideline can be a useful method for lining a bank account in hard economic times.

This book is going to talk about one very successful and quite easy way to make cash, once you know the ins and outs and the general basics.

Have you heard of Craigslist?

Craigslist is a hugely popular auction selling website, which allows people to sell their unwanted items locally, without having to worry about the problems associated with shipping and sending items cross country, or even internationally. There are many auction reselling sites out there, and even pages and boards on social media sites, such as Facebook. Whilst these are useful, there are some downsides associated with selling on eBay especially - namely fees.

In many ways, Craigslist is a little like eBay, but without the fees and without the hassle. For this reason, many people are using Craigslist as a way to make extra cash, and not just for selling items they don't want. You do not need to pay fees when you sell something on Craigslist, but you do on eBay, and the more you sell the item for, the higher the fees. You also don't need to box up the item and ship it to the person's address, never sure if it has actually arrived in one piece. Craigslist is a local site, and therefore collections are done in person, either from a house (not the most recommended option) or form a mutually convenient pickup point. From a safety point of view, mutual public pick up points are best.

How can you make cash by reselling items on this popular selling site? This book is going to answer that exact question and show you how to do it from scratch. By the end of this book, you'll be ready and excited to get started on your own reselling business. Whilst profits might not come to you in abundance straight away, with a little time building up your reselling business, you'll find more gains coming your way.

What is Reselling?

Reselling on Craigslist can be done in two distinct ways.

- Firstly, you run a business selling items to buyers, sourcing your items from outside businesses, e.g. trade manufacturers or other auction sites. You can choose to have a stock which you sell, or you can source as and when a sale takes place. This is a more difficult way to resell items on Craigslist.

- Secondly, you purchase an item from Craigslist and sell it on for a higher price. This option is the best way to get started with reselling, and sourcing out bargains will no doubt become an addiction!

Both options involve finding a niche which has demand. For instance, perhaps in your local area, you find that cellphone accessories sell very well. In this case, you would purchase cellphone cases for a low price and you would sell them on for a higher cost, making a profit in the process. You can then grow your business by branching out to other associated items, such as laptop accessories, phone chargers, etc. Whilst you're probably never going to become a millionaire from reselling on Craigslist, you can certainly make a tidy profit every month.

How much? You could make between $300 - 700 per month. That's the same amount as a part-time job! For that reason, we're going to class reselling on Craigslist as a passive income method, i.e. you're making money with not much effort, and you could even do it on the side, alongside your regular full time or another part-time job.

How This Book Will Help You

This book is a from scratch guide on how to become a quality reseller on Craigslist. There is more to this subject than you will first realize, and it's very similar to starting your own business.

To stop your reselling becoming a hindrance to the rest of your life, e.g. encroaching on your own time or your primary job, you need to arrange your time and plan everything carefully. If you can do this, you will find that reselling on Craigslist will bring you profits with little effort, and it could even become an enjoyable hobby!

We will take about what it takes to become a reseller, the pros and cons, how to arrange your time, and how to find a product which sells well. At the end of the book, you will also find a bonus chapter. This chapter is an interview with a computer hardware reseller who has made a tidy profit from reselling on Craigslist. This shows you just how much of a reality this all can be, and you'll also be able to find out useful information, with insider hints and tips.

So, enough procrastination, let's get started on learning more about reselling on Craigslist, before diving into the specifics.

Chapter 1: Why do You Want to be a Reseller on Craigslist?

First things first, why should you become a reseller on Craigslist? It's no good starting something if you're not sure what is in it for you! You also need to have a clear view of what reselling is, and what it is going to involve.

Craigslist reselling isn't a difficult process once you know what your niche area is going to be. The difficulty comes in when you are identifying what you are going to sell and how you're going to sell it. You need to choose a product, or a range of products, which you are sure has a demand. For instance, purchasing a range of antiques and expecting to sell them in an area which is not so affluent for a high price is unrealistic. On the other hand, if you live in an area which has a high amount of teenagers or youngsters, then the cell phone accessory route is more than likely going to bring you profits.

It's about knowing your area, knowing the people who live there, and understanding what they like and don't like. You also need to make sure that you don't choose prices which are far too high. If you can do your research and work all of this out before you begin, you'll find your business flourishes quite quickly. On the other hand, if you jump in feet first, you're likely to stumble a few times before you find your feet.

Research and planning are key!

The Benefits of Reselling on Craigslist

In order to pursue something, you need to know you're going to benefit from it! We don't work for anything, and whilst Craigslist reselling isn't a particularly in-depth or difficult process, it still takes time and effort to some degree.

Let's explore the main benefits of reselling on Craigslist.

Extra Income

Let's start with the most obvious of reasons. Reselling items on Craigslist can bring extra cash your way. The more you sell, the more money you make, and the more you learn about the reselling process, the more accurate you will become on your pricing. A little later in this book, we're going to talk about tips to maximize your sales, and therefore bring extra cash and exposure your way. The more people you reach, the more chances you have of making cash!

The first time you make a sale on Craigslist, it's likely to be a low amount, however, you need to cast your net quite wide at first. If you can do this, and if you can be persistent, you will notice greater gains.

Many people choose to use reselling on Craigslist as a passive income method. This is something you can do on the side, in your spare time, which doesn't take up a huge amount of your time after the initial set up stage. Other possible passive income methods include renting out a home you own, and receiving rental payments from tenants every month, dabbling in the stock market, affiliate marketing through blogging, and writing a book and selling it for royalties. None of these methods have no effort involved, and the first set up process will take time, but after that, they basically run themselves.

Whilst Craigslist reselling isn't completely hands-off, it does take minimal time once you manage to streamline your own process and create a business flow which suits your time and your needs.

You Meet a Range of People

The good thing about Craigslist is that it isn't impersonal, e.g. you get to actually meet the person you're selling to, and you have communication with them over the phone or via email. This means you're going to inevitably meet people you don't want to, of course, but it also means you get to meet new people who you might click with too. You never know, you could meet a new friend through your reselling endeavors!

We touched upon safety a little earlier on, and because Craigslist reselling hinges on in-person meetings to pass the item over and transfer the money, you do have to be more careful than you would be if you were using a site like eBay. The lack of time spent parceling up items and sending them to an address is at the expense of your time, i.e. you need to go and meet the person.

You should always ensure that you meet in the day time, in a public place, and that you don't arrange for anyone to pick items up from your home address, or that you go to an address you do not know. Of course, there are going to be times when at-home pickups can't be avoided, e.g. for large items. In this case, never go alone, and never be home alone when the person visits. Simply use your common sense and know that whilst person might seem wonderfully friendly on the phone or on email, safety must come first.

That is the grim side of the coin, however, and for the most part, Craigslist reselling is a great opportunity to meet new people and learn about their lives and stories. You're basically getting socializing and business all rolled into one!

It's Good Fun

If you can create a way of working which is enjoyable, you'll find your reselling business to be quite fun. It will feel like more of a hobby than a job, and that's a great way to earn extra cash. It won't feel like work, because it's really not!

The crux of this point is that you need to ensure you organize your time well and that it doesn't become something you can't keep up with, or don't have the time for. Provided you do have the time and you do your research into what is going to work and what won't, you'll enjoy reselling on Craigslist, and it will create a fun sideline job for you.

It's a Way to Fill Your Spare Time

Look at it this way - you can either spend your spare time doing nothing constructive, perhaps even spending money you don't really have, or you can do something which is worthwhile and earns you some cash. Reselling on Craigslist is fun if you have the time, so if you are working part-time, or perhaps not working at all, you will find this to be a fun way to fill your spare time, and it will keep you away from other things which would cost money. Surely that's more useful?

Offers Freedom Away From The Office

If you can really make Craigslist reselling work for you, it will give you an official break from being stuck in an office. For those who manage to make a wage equivalent to that of a part-time job, you have total freedom to organize your time however you like. You are in effect your own boss and you don't have to answer to anyone.

If you have other demands on your time, e.g. a young family, you're caring for someone, or you have other responsibilities which you need to attend to, you can easily arrange your reselling endeavors around these things, without it becoming too much, or encroaching on the things you need to fit into your time.

In addition, you are not sat cooped up in an office, factory, or another working establishment, as you can work from anywhere, provided you have an Internet connection! You could even sit in your local cafe and work through your emails and list your new items.

Opportunities For Growth

If you organize your business well, there is a lot of room for growth here. You can start off with one item and see how that goes, monitoring sales and looking for trends. From there you can branch out into associated items, which are a little different but still have a link. A little earlier we mentioned selling cell phone cases and covers, and an associated product could be chargers or laptop cases, etc. There is a lot of scope for growth provided you do your research and learn which products are likely to sell well, versus the ones which won't.

These are the specific benefits of reselling on Craigslist, but you might even find a few more benefits that we haven't mentioned. You get out of it what you put in, and the more you focus your time, the more you will be able to make money-wise, and the greater enjoyment you will get out of your new endeavors. Look at it as a business and you'll focus your time and attention much more easily. Despite that, don't let it become a drag, and always keep enjoyment to the forefront of your mind. If you can do that, you'll win on all sides.

Chapter 2: What do You Need to Become a Reseller on Craigslist?

Now you know what reselling is, and you know what the benefits are, let's now talk about the things you'll need in order to make it all work.

There are six main elements you need to become a reseller on Craigslist, some physical and some more about mindset. Let's explore them in turn.

You Need a Computer/Tablet

These days you can do most things on a smartphone, but if you're going to be serious about making your reselling work for you, you should invest in a laptop, desktop, or at least a tablet. This will make it easier for you to look at prices, find items to sell, and list for yourself. You'll also be able to answer emails much more easily, and as a result, you won't miss any emails.

You can organize yourself much better on a computer, and if you want to keep your business ticking along, without receiving a bad reputation for not being up to date with communication, this is a vital part of the puzzle.

A laptop or tablet is probably preferable to a desktop PC because you have more freedom when you can move around. We mentioned earlier about doing some work from a coffee shop, or even in the park on a sunny day, and that is not at all possible with a large desktop computer! A laptop is ideal.

You Need a Reliable Internet Connection

You can't resell anything on Craigslist without an Internet connection, so make sure that you have WIFI or mobile Internet at the very least. You can easily set up a mobile Internet hotspot from your cell phone and use that, but you will be using your data. Again, coffee shops are ideal, because the WIFI is normally free!

You also need to be relatively free to answer emails when they come in, to avoid buyers waiting for too long for their answers. If you wait until the next day, they might have changed their mind and gone elsewhere. We're not suggesting you need to be connected 24/7, but the ability to check a few times a day is essential.

You Need a Phone

Buyers can decide whether to contact you via the telephone or via email. Some may prefer a more personal touch, and that way they can get their questions answered much quicker. For that reason, you need to have a cell phone which you can answer easily. Most people already have this, so it's not the biggest deal, but it is certainly something to bear in mind and consider.

Life Will be Easier if You Have a Car

Whilst it's not impossible to do your drop-offs without a car, you will find it much easier if you do. We are certainly not suggesting you go out to buy a car just for your reselling plans, but if you have one already, that is certainly going to make everything easier.

Craigslist is built on the idea that you are selling locally, and not having to send things via cargo or the regular post. This means the ability to meet people in mutually convenient places. Because you are providing a service, you should be able to reach most places in the local area, within reason. It's unreasonable to expect a buyer to travel a fair distance without transport when you are the one offering them the purchasing service. It is more towards the seller's side when it comes to how far to travel. Despite that, always remember safety.

There are going to be some items which simply cannot be taken to a place for collection, e.g. large items, but if you are going to specialize in large items, you need to come to an arrangement which is both safe and convenient for you in terms of pick-ups and drop offs.

A Passion For Searching For Great Deals on Craigslist or Elsewhere

You need to find the items you're going to resell somewhere and Craigslist is a great place to start! You can do these one of two ways. You can spend your time looking for real bargains on Craigslist and then resell them on when you receive them, or you can have a stock of items which you have sourced from elsewhere, e.g. trade sellers. It's up to you how you do it because both ways are classed as reselling.

Whichever option you go for, you need to dedicate yourself to finding those bargains to be able to resell on. We mentioned that reselling on Craigslist is a good passive income method, but it does require some work, and it isn't simply something which runs itself. If you can organize your time and enjoy looking for deals, you'll find it all much easier. If you hate searching for items to purchase and resell, you're not going to get optimum enjoyment out of your time and you're not going to find much pleasure in this business.

A Good Understanding of Market Prices

You also need to have a good understanding of how much things are selling for, and how low or high you can really go without your item being left unsold. This is something you will pick up much easier over time, but the first few times you need to be able to work with estimates. A good understanding of the market will help to establish your reselling efforts, so put some time into searching around on Craigslist for current listings, plus look at other sites, such as eBay, to give you another side of the coin.

If you list your items too high, nobody is going to buy them. If you list your items too low, you're not going to make a profit. Neither is a good option, and you need to find the necessary piece of positive middle ground. Research is the single best way to achieve that.

As you can see, you don't really need a whole lot to get started, but one thing we haven't mentioned is the items you want to sell! These will come to you as you get into the purchasing and reselling way of life. You are going to find items from other places, e.g. source items to resell on from wholesalers or other sellers, then you need to make sure that you establish positive and reliable relationships with those companies. You also need to make sure that you are certainly going to make a profit and sell the items, otherwise, you will be left out of pocket. Again, you'll know that by the market research you do.

Chapter 3: Reselling for Beginners

Now let's get practical!

You now know all the background information on reselling on Craigslist, but what you don't know yet is a step by step guide on how to source your first item and resell it. We are going to cover that in detail in our next chapter, but this chapter is going to give you plenty of hints and tips on what to do and what not to do. By avoiding pitfalls, you can create a much more likely to succeed picture.

We're going to assume that you're going to go down the easiest route of reselling, i.e. finding deals on Craigslist and selling them on. If you are going to source your items from elsewhere, the general way to do it will be the same, but you will need to find your items from the sources you find most reliable. That is something you will need to research and build up over time.

Stick to One Item First of All

It's best to stick to one item and not to overwhelm yourself with a million different items. If you do that you're not going to be sure who is calling or emailing about which item, and you're going to end up with more items than you know what to do with. This is when problems and mistakes happen. Stick to one item at a time and you will not only find it easier, but you'll also be able to minimize issues. As you become more experienced over time, you can try a few at one time, but for starters, stick to one niche and one item at a time.

For instance, if you are selling a Samsung cell phone, you would list that item, complete the process, field enquiries about it, and then hopefully sell it. You would then take it to the meeting place, swap the item for the cash, and then start your next cycle of searching for items and reselling. This is the single easiest way to start. Many people also choose to stick to this method, but if you want to add a few more into the mix as you become more experienced, that is something you will be able to do as confidence builds.

Also, Stick to One Group of Items

We talked earlier about finding out which items will sell well in your particular area and which don't have the greatest demand. It is best to stick to one particular niche, e.g. the cell phone case example we gave earlier. This will allow you to become an expert in that area, you'll understand market prices, and you then have scope for growth in the future.

If you start buying any old item, how can you be sure you're getting a good deal? You can't be an expert in all fields! You can branch out in the future, but for now, specializing is the best way forward. By becoming an expert in that particular area, you can see deals easier, you can sidestep issues easier, and you'll also find it much easier to make a profit overall.

Keep Accurate And Up-To-Date Records

It's impossible to be able to tell if something is working for you or not if you don't record things. By records, we are talking about keeping a note of how much you have bought and how much you have sold. This will help you identify if you need to cut back on your buying for a while until you've managed to sell a few items, or whether you can continue to search for deals. Basically, you can tell if you are breaking even, and how much of a profit is coming your way. If you're noticing less in the way of success, they can look to tweak how you are working and improve what you are doing.

These records don't need to be super in-depth, and they don't need to be official, just a list of things you've bought with a running total, versus the things you've sold. That will give you all the information you need. Keep it simple and don't overcomplicate matters.

Know Your Rights And The Rights of The Buyer

Craigslist doesn't tend to get involved in any sales unless there is a major dispute going on. The single best piece of advice is to solve any issues which arise between you and a buyer because if you don't, your reputation will basically go south. In this case, word will get around and you will not be able to sell as well in the future.

Again, think of your reselling hobby as a business. Every business needs to pay attention to its reputation and market its services in a positive way. Therefore, large businesses have dedicated customer services departments - because the customer needs to be listened to, and they need to have their grievances ironed out. If they don't, sales will be affected and therefore profits will be lower.

Never underestimate the power of the reputation in any part of life, especially when it comes to sales. Nobody is going to want to purchase items from someone who has a bad reputation, and who has been known in the past to not listen to their buyers, or not care about issues which arose. Nobody is going to care whether or not you were in the right or the buyer, they will simply see the issue and decide to go elsewhere.

Think about your own experiences with buyers, perhaps on eBay. If you saw that they had less than a perfect score, did you purchase from them? Probably not. If you did, you probably thought twice about it beforehand. Don't let that happen and simply communicate well and iron out any problems when they arise. It will be worth it in the long-run.

Safety Comes First

We mentioned this one previously, but it is so important that we need to highlight it again. Most people on this planet are honest, hard-working, and reliable people. Some, however, are not. You have no idea if the person you are meeting is in the latter or former category. Do not take risks. The best safety guidelines to follow are:

- Always meet in public places
- Always meet in daylight - midday and early afternoon are good times as there are more people around
- If the weather is bad and causing it to be dark and miserable, arrange for another time or meet somewhere indoors and public
- Cafes and restaurants are good places to meet, as are shopping malls
- If you feel nervous, make sure you take someone with you
- Never give a buyer your home address and ask them to come and pick up the item
- Never go to a buyer's address to drop an item off
- If for some reason you have no choice but to meet in a place which isn't as public as you would like, do not go alone - take someone you trust with you

It's common sense at the end of the day, but it can be easy to throw it out of the window and trust too easily. The kind and helpful person you are speaking to on the phone or via email may seem fine, but you do not know how they are in reality. The same advice goes for when you are purchasing items from Craigslist, in order to sell on.

Keep Reality in Your Mind When Looking For Deals

It can be very easy to let your mind run away with you and end up trying to buy items which in reality are not going to sell as well. Always keep your plan in mind and your common sense to the front of everything. At the end of the day, you are trying to make a profit, not a loss! As with our first point, stick to one niche which you know very well and you shouldn't go too far wrong.

Understand That it Might Take Time

It might not happen overnight for you, and you need to be fine with that fact. Miracles don't happen in seconds, remember! Persevere for a while, but if you find it isn't working, it could very well be that you simply need to change your niche or look at your pricing. There is no real reason why reselling items on Craigslist will fail, and if you're not making a profit, it's probably something quite easy which needs to be tweaked.

These are a few things you simply need to keep in mind when you start out on your reselling journey.

Chapter 4: The Five Important Tasks When Reselling on Craigslist

Reselling on Craigslist can easily be broken down into five easy tasks. It's that simple - just five tasks which you need to complete well, in order to find deals and sell them on for a profit.

We have broken it down into these easy steps because the whole process of reselling can seem quite overwhelming at first. This is simply because you are not familiar with it yet. Once you know what you're doing, it will seem like child's play.

The single best way to conduct reselling in the most efficient way is to research the process, familiarize yourself with it, practice once in a slow manner, and then ensure that you tie up any loose ends before moving forward with the next sale. When searching for deals, always make sure that you think twice before purchasing, and ask yourself whether it will make a realistic resale, for a good price.

This chapter is going to take you through the process of buying an item and reselling it, step by step. Print this chapter out and keep it as your guide throughout your first few attempts at reselling on Craigslist. After that, you'll be doing it with your eyes closed.

The process is:

1. Browse Craigslist to find deals and purchase the ones which make sense
2. Writing a quality advertisement for the item and reviewing it before posting
3. Taking quality pictures of the item, including any faults
4. Communicating with the person you are either buying or selling from
5. Driving or taking transportation to pick up the item

Of course, there are smaller tasks to complete the full step, but breaking it down into the smallest number of steps possible, makes the whole process less daunting.

Step 1 - Browse Craigslist to Find Deals

The first step is finding something to actually sell! At this point, you need to spend some time browsing Craigslist and looking for deals. The key point here is knowing the type of times you want to sell, i.e. your target niche. This will make finding deals easier because you can look in one or two categories, and not have to browse the entirety of the site.

Craigslist is arranged in product categories, e.g. jewelry, clothing, computer hardware, etc, and the list of categories is quite extensive. Before you begin looking for deals, deciding upon your niche is vital, if you want to be more time constructive. It will take you endless hours if you have no clue what types of things you want to resell because you'll have to look at everything. Do you know how many items are listed on Craigslist within one region every day? A lot!

Make your life easier and know what you want before you start.

From there, it's about browsing and knowing the market price. Again, this is something to research before you begin. It's a good idea to spend a few hours really digging into the ads which you see already listed and comprising prices. You could also do some cross-over work with eBay and other auction sites, to see if the same kind of marketing prices are evident. If not, you can see if the products already listed on Craigslist or too high, or too low, and come to the best price for you to buy the product and then ultimately resell it for. This will give you important information on how much you should offer because of course, you want to make a profit - that's the whole point!

Once you've found something you want to buy, reach out to the seller and make contact. You can do this either by email or telephone, whichever option they have mentioned on the ad, and whatever you are comfortable with too. Most people prefer telephone because it is more personal and much faster, but other people prefer emails because there is an electronic paper trail of evidence, so you can look back over what was said, where to meet, etc.

Only buy one item at a time at first. This will cut down on the chances of possibly losing out by making a profit margin loss, and will make life easier in terms of knowing which items are currently on your sales list.

It is perfectly acceptable to place an offer on the item and not offer to pay the full price, but do bear in mind that the person may say 'no'. For this reason, don't offer a wildly low price as you're simply going to insult them and they will not sell the item to you! A little lower than the asking price is sensible, and you can banter back and forth and reach an agreement from there.

Step 2 - Write a Quality Advertisement For Item You're Reselling

Now you have the item in your hands, you need to work to resell it. The first step is writing a quality advertisement and reviewing it, to check it includes all necessary details. It is best to cut down on the number of questions which buyers may ask you, to avoid everything becoming confusing and slow. The best way to do this is to anticipate questions and answer them in your ad.

As a bare minimum you should mention the following:

- The name of the item
- Specs, e.g. year, any functions or specific information related to the item
- Photos (more on that shortly)
- The price - it is always better to ask for more than you're willing to accept, but not wildly so. By doing this, you are giving yourself room for bartering, as buyers will always ask

to purchase for less. If you ask for more, you're not losing out on what you know you can get for the item
- A reason why you are selling
- A short description, which is concise and to the point

Your ad needs to be friendly but professional. Do not simply list features with bullet points and leave it at that, as this doesn't come over as particularly useful to buyers. Do not speak too much but simply be concise with the information the buyer needs to know. You should mention the reason for selling because it helps to build the bond of trust with the buyer. If they know you're simply selling it because you have no use for it anymore, they're more likely to be attracted to the item than if you don't mention it. In this case, they may think there is something wrong with it.

Always re-read your advertisement before posting it - bad grammar and spelling mistakes a very off-putting to many people!

Step 3 - Take Quality Photographs

This is a very important step. Make sure you take at least two quality photographs of the item and post them with your add. More than one photograph is always recommended because it gives the buyer more information. Obviously, you should take photos from different angles, to give the buyer a greater idea of what they are purchasing.

If there are any faults with the item, make sure you take photos of those too. You should also describe these in detail in your ad description - honestly is vital as your reputation will be damaged if you hide any important details.

Make sure the item is clean when you take the photos and that the background is clear, e.g. no items from your home that make the photo look unprofessional. It is best to move the item closer to a window or light in order to take the photo, as it will be clearer for the buyer to see the item up-close.

Step 4 - Communicating With The Buyer or Seller

At this point, you either want to buy an item, or someone has contacted you and is interested in purchasing the item you have listed. Either way, politeness and professionalism are vital.

You can either be contacted by email or telephone, and you should answer any queries you get as quickly as you can. This doesn't mean you need to answer every email within minutes, but it does mean checking your inbox a few times a day, to make sure you don't miss anything important. If you notice you have missed call on your phone, make sure you call them back as soon as it is convenient. Failure to do this potentially means a missed sale or purchase.

Make sure communication is clear. For instance, make sure you cover the basics:

- Answer any questions they have about the product
- Arrange the price
- Confirm that you will be receiving the money in cash, upon receipt of the item
- Arrange how you are going to get the item to them, e.g. arrange a mutually convenient meeting place in public, in daylight hours
- Confirm the drop once more before the arranged time

If there are any queries or concerns which happen after the sale, e.g. after you have taken the item to the person and they have paid you, make sure you iron these out as quickly as you can. Whilst the sale is officially over by this point, not answering someone's problems post-sale could land you with a poor reputation, as we explored in further detail a little easier on in the book.

Step 5 - Taking The Item to The Buyer/Picking up The Item

The rules for taking a sold item to a buyer, and picking up a deal you've found from a seller are the same. Safety is key!

Arrange a mutually convenient place to meet, and make sure that it is during daylight and in a public place. If you can meet somewhere like a shopping mall or a restaurant/coffee shop, this is going to be better than meeting on the street. We talked a lot earlier about safety, so simply heed these rules, but also make sure that the pickup or collection point is somewhere you can both easily reach.

Once more, it will be better if you have a car and your own transportation, however, if not you can use public transport, provided the item isn't too large.

This is the point where you hand over the cash, or the cash is handed to you. For buying and selling on Craigslist, payment by cash is always preferred. Never give your bank details to anyone, i.e. for them to put the money into your account. If the sale is for a large amount and cash simply isn't feasible, you can ask to use PayPal. This is a better option because you simply use the email address linked to your account, and you get a much safer experience as a result. Signing up for a PayPal account is also free, so if the buyer doesn't have one currently and the sale is for a large amount, it isn't too much of an issue to sign up and fix the transaction.

Once more - never give out your bank details and never use any third-party payment transaction other than PayPal. Cash is always the single best option.

And that is really it! That is your process of reselling on Craigslist, and as you can see, it's not a critically difficult process overall. For the first few times, it is going to take you longer because you need to gain experience of finding deals and also writing quality ads which are going to attract buyers to your items. Once you have more experience in doing that, you will find it faster and easier to list items.

Chapter 5: The Importance of Time Management & Planning

When you decide you are going to place effort and time into reselling on Craigslist, you need to organize yourself from the get-go. This will ensure that you overcome any hurdles faster, and hopefully, avoid them in the first place. It also means that you are much less likely to notice your reselling efforts encroaching on your own time and space.

First things first, how much do you want to make? Every business (and that's how you need to treat it) needs and aim. If you know a general amount of how much you want to recoup back, you'll be able to work towards that goal with more motivation than otherwise. Without an idea of how much you want to gain in profit, you're going to be bumbling around from sale to sale and not really noticing your gains.

Be realistic in this number, because at first, you might not notice the greatest profit coming your way. It may take time. Perhaps you will be lucky, i.e. you'll find some fantastic deals from the get-go and be able to rack up a tidy profit from your first few sales. It is possible, but it's always best to be realistic and aim for lower amounts, to begin with. Once your experience grows, you'll also notice your profits growing too.

We mentioned earlier that it is possible to make between $300 - 700 per month from reselling on Craigslist. For your first few months, perhaps aim for the $300 mark and see how you go. Make sure that you review your efforts as you move along and then give yourself a higher aim for the following month. This will push you to keep finding those deals and keeping selling items on. Before you know it, you'll be earning a part-time wage without even realizing it!

How to Manage Your Time Effectively

We've mentioned this phrase already, but the single best way to be organized and successful is to treat your reselling as a business. In many ways that is what it is. At its very core, business is something you spend time on and earn money from. That is what you are doing, so therefore you have a business!

At first, you need to do your homework and familiarize yourself with Craigslist, so it makes perfect sense that in the initial part, you're going to spend more time on your efforts. Once you purchase your first item and start reselling it is important to have boundaries. Do not dedicate your entire time to reselling on Craigslist. If you do that, and if you begin to treat it like a real job, you're not going to enjoy it. There is a difference between treating it as a business and treating it as a job. It should be a business you enjoy, not something you have to do otherwise you don't get paid!

Look at the time you have available and dedicate a set amount. Make sure that amount is reasonable, and that it isn't eating into all your spare time. Reselling on Craigslist shouldn't take too much of your time, and once you establish yourself and become more experienced, you'll notice that it takes an hour or two at the very most every day. On most days it will probably be even less.

It might be a good idea to note down how much time you are spending on it at first, so you can check that it isn't taking over your life. Time planning will help your reselling efforts remain enjoyable and profitable.

Keep Your Expectations Realistic

Of course, you want to make as much profit as you can, that is human nature and the very reason why you wanted to learn more about reselling on Craigslist, but you need to be realistic, otherwise you will fail from the start. You cannot buy something for $100 and expect to sell it on for three times that amount. Generally speaking, you can expect to make a profit of between 30-50% on the price you paid. That's not a bad amount!

There may be times when you grab a real bargain and resell it for a very tidy profit, but make peace with the fact that these occasions are likely to be very few and far between. If you keep your profit expectations realistic, you won't be disappointed and you will still line your profit coffers very handsomely.

By knowing what to expect when reselling on Craigslist, you will find it much easier to navigate your first sale. Information is power when it comes to dealing with sales and the public. Whilst most sellers and buyers you will come into contact with are honest and simply after a good price for an item they want, some may not be quite so honest. Being open to the fact that there may be scams here and there will help you know what to look for. A few red flags include:

- Unwillingness to speak on the phone, and only wants communication via email - This isn't always a sign of something amiss, but it can be in some circumstances
- Doesn't want to pay cash or use PayPal and tries to coerce you into payment via some other means
- You simply don't feel right about the transaction - sometimes listening to your gut is the best way forward
- They have bad feedback or a bad reputation in general

Listen to your inner voice and if something doesn't seem right, it's completely fine to pass on that sale or purchase and look for another. Your safety and your finances are not things you should gamble with. Overall, however, the overwhelming numbers of resales on Craigslist are easy, quick, and go without the slightest hitch.

Chapter 6: Secrets Tips to Boost Your Selling Power

We have gone through the process of reselling items on Craigslist and you now know the overall steps to take, but what about the hidden hints you can use to boost your selling power and ensure good quality and profitable sale?

Much of time, you will learn things as you go along, from experience, but it is also worth listening to advice from those in the know. Below you'll find a few secrets to help you make better sales, but remember to always follow the procedure through carefully, and to stick to the safety guidelines we talked about more than once in this book already. Those are the true basics, and any successful venture needs to have the basics covered carefully. After that, you can add boosts to give you a better experience and outcome.

Tip 1 - When Selling, Think Like a Buyer

You should never simply see your sales from a seller's point of view. Thinking like a buyer will help you to cover all bases and have a better selling outcome. For instance, why should they buy from you and not someone else? What makes you stand out? Why are you a better option? Make yourself stand out, give them something that nobody else does, e.g. high-quality customer service or a warranty after purchase. The small things make a huge difference and will help you to stand head and shoulders over your competition.

There are always going to be other sellers in the same niche as you, and they will be trying to outdo you at the same time. Thinking like a buyer will give you more information, and it will give you a different viewpoint on which to build your success.

Tip 2 - Cover All Bases in Your Advertisement

When writing your ad, make sure you have covered as much information as possible. Think about the questions buyers might ask, and thinking like a buyer (as in tip 1) will allow you to identify the things which might be asked of you. By doing this, you're cutting down on the time it takes for a sale to work, and it also makes the buyer trust you more, because you're knowledgeable and gives them what they need.

Think about times in the past when you have wanted to buy something. Of course, you wanted to find out the information you needed without having to ask a million questions. This simply looks more professional. You should also think about the time it takes for emails to ping back and forth with questions. Even phone calls can take time if you miss one or two at first.

Draft your advertisement first and then re-read it. You could even review it in line with another similar advert and see if you have covered the same bases, and then add extra information to make yourself stand out.

Tip 3 - Make Sure Your Photos Are High Quality

Check your photos before you upload them and look for any potential issues. For instance, is the item clean? Can you see items in the background that don't need to be there? Can you see the time clearly? Is the lighting sufficient? If you want to make a professional business out of your reselling endeavors, you need to make sure that the photos you show to people are equally as professional.

You don't need to purchase a specific quality camera to take these photos, as smartphones these days tend to have very quality picture taking facilities, but do make sure that the lighting is enough for the buyer to be able to check and really assess what they're buying. Remember, this isn't like in a shop when you can pick the item up and look at it for yourself. Whilst the buyer can ask to see the item when you go to meet to drop it off, by that point the sale is generally confirmed. Give the buyer all the visual information they need and you'll find more sales come your way as a result.

Tip 4 - Is The Sale Really Worth it?

Not every sale will be worth your time or effort. For instance, if someone from a rural area wants to purchase your item and it is going to take you far too long to get to the collection point and cost more in gas than the profit you're going to make, you need to think carefully about whether or not to proceed.

Reselling is not supposed to be a problem or a hindrance to your time, so if a sale looks like it is heading that way, you are within your rights to tell the buyer that you aren't willing to sell to them because of this very reason. Always tell them why, and don't leave it until the last minute, as that is common courtesy.

Your profit margin should be at least 20% from any sale you make, and that the lowest margin you should accept. Anything less than that and you are moving into territory which simply isn't worth your time or effort. At first, you might be worried about passing up sales, but doing so gives you the opportunity to make a more profitable sale in the near future.

Another thing to look at in terms of whether a sale is worth it or not is whether the profit margin is going to be enough. For instance, we just mentioned that the minimum 20% profit is what you should be looking for, but if you buy an item for $20, your 20% profit is only going to be $4. Is that worth your time? Probably not, but this is something to think carefully about, especially when searching for deals on Craigslist in the first place.

Tip 5 - Give Great Customer Service

People are much more likely to buy from you again if they had a good experience. Part of that is giving great customer service, even to those who simply contact you to ask a question about a product and don't actually end up buying it.

Always be friendly, always answer emails and calls, and always treat your buyers as you would want to be treated. Remember, you're treating your reselling as a business, and customer service is vital in any line of business.

We're not suggesting that you would be anything other than polite and friendly, but sometimes if you answer a call in a rush, e.g. you're in the supermarket and your phone rings, it's easy to be a little brusque. You certainly don't mean to be, but the buyer could take your attitude the wrong way and as a result, the sale doesn't go ahead. It's not this single sale that could be affected either, as in the future that person might see your name and not think to contact you about another item. They may even tell their friends not to buy from you. Remember, Craigslist is a local service, and word of mouth gets around very easily indeed.

Customer service is a very easy subject to cover, which makes it a no-brainer to tick it off your list. For instance, all you need to do is:

- Be professional
- Be friendly
- Be helpful
- Answer calls and emails
- Do what you promise you will do
- Be on time when you meet, and always be early if possible

It's that simple! It's about basic common courtesy, and if you can remember this whilst you're in the middle of trying to resell items and make cash, you'll find that more cash comes your way from sales overall.

Tip 6 - Build up a Bond of Trust With Your Buyers

Customer service and trust are two things which overlap, but trust is important enough to have a mention of its own. Your buyer needs to trust that you are giving them what they expect and that you are honest and open about the product. This is a baseline requirement and something you would expect from buying items from another seller yourself.

Again, look at this as a business. If you were to buy an item from a large supermarket, you automatically trust that you're getting what you pay for. This is because you trust that supermarket and you know that any problem you encounter would be sorted out quickly. This is the same kind of feel you're going for with your reselling efforts.

Building trust can take time, but it's not difficult. Giving great customer service is one way to go about this because you're instantly putting that person at ease. Feeling comfortable with a seller is one way for a buyer to feel that they trust you. There are a few other ways of doing this too:

- **Give your telephone number and not just your email** - Whilst it's completely acceptable to want to communicate solely by email, it does look a little 'off' in some ways. For instance, scammers will certainly not give out a telephone number and will only ever speak to potential buyers with email. Whilst you might have a completely honest reason for not wanting to give your telephone number out, the buyer may see it a different way. Be completely transparent and that trust bond will be easier to achieve.
- **Provide a small warranty if you are selling electronic items** - This isn't only limited to electronics, but this is the group of items which is probably the most risk-ridden. Electronics can break or go wrong at any time, and it probably has nothing to do with you or the way you handled it. To cut down on the risk and give your buyer more peace of mind, offer a warranty for one week after the sale. This will help them to see that there is nothing wrong with the item you're selling, and you're not hiding anything. The chances are the warranty will never be used, but the fact you're offering it looks positive.
- **Give a reason for selling in your advertisement** - Another way to help a buyer feel more comfortable and trusting, especially if you are selling electronics or large items, is to

give the reason why you are selling in your advertisement. If you don't do this, they might automatically think that there is something wrong with it, and you're trying to offload it for a profit. This isn't the case, so simply say that the item 'is in perfect condition, but is simply no longer used/no longer needed'. That is enough and is open and honest.
- **Always be friendly and professional** - The same as the customer service route, but being honest and open, professional and friendly shows the buyer that you are not scamming them, you are not hiding anything, and that they can trust your professionalism.

These are quick and easy tips you can use to boost your selling power and make your buyers feel more comfortable and at ease with your services. Remember, reputation is everything, and the better your reputation, the more likely you are to receive repeat sales in the future. Also, be sure to sort out any issues as they arise, and not to simply fly off the radar or not speak to the buyer once the sale has concluded. Most disputes are very easily sorted out and by doing so quickly, you're pleasing the buyer and ensuring that they will recommend you in the future.

Conclusion

And there we have it! You now know all there is to know about reselling on Craigslist and how to make a profit. When done correctly, reselling could certainly give you a substantial amount of spare cash every month. You could even decide to do this as a part-time job, alongside another job, or to bring extra cash to your bank account.

The hope is that by this point you're feeling much more relaxed about the process and more confident that you can make a success of this too. At first, it probably seemed like a mountain to deal with, but reselling is actually not that difficult. The key is finding deals to sell on in the first place, or sourcing goods from outside companies or manufacturers which you're sure you can resell for a good enough profit. Yes, it takes time at first, but as you become more experienced and more confident, you will find that you develop an instinct for a deal or bargain, and the selling side of things will become second nature.

This conclusion isn't the end of the story, however, as if you continue reading you'll find a bonus chapter, packed with information you can use to make your own business a major success. We've spoken to a successful power reseller in Vancouver, who has made a full-time job out of selling computer hardware. Through this Q&A session, you'll learn about how he started, how he built up his business, and how he runs it on a daily basis. Knowledge is power in this regard, and his huge success should be your inspiration!

Of course, we mentioned that it is entirely possible to make a part-time income of between $300 - 700 by reselling items on Craigslist, but it's not out of the question to push the bar further and make more. Our Q&A stands as a testament to that fact! Hopefully, you'll find plenty of inspiration to grow your own business.

There is one item we need to mention about once more, purely because of its sheer importance - safety.

Whenever you're dealing with the general public and people you don't know, you have to be on your guard, especially in this day and age. Whilst the vast majority of people you come into contact with will be completely honest and have good intentions, there are a very small minority of people who are simply trying to make a quick buck. You also have to be on your guard about general personal safety too, because you're going to be meeting these people in person.

Yet again - never visit a house or have anyone come to your home. If you have no choice, e.g. the item is so large it's impossible to take it to a mutual meeting place, make sure someone is home with you, or take a person to the buyer's home. It might sound like an overreaction and being very untrusting, but it's always better to be safe than sorry. Anyone buying an item from you will want the same kind of protection because safety works both ways. It's likely that if your buyer is a sensible person and you have to take the item to their home, they will also have someone at home with them because they don't know you too!

The vast majority of sales and purchases on Craigslist will be items which can be taken to a mutually convenient collection or drop off point. A few places which are ideal for meetings include shopping malls, restaurants, and coffee shops. If you don't want to hang around and you have other places to be, the inside of a shopping mall is a good idea. You could opt for just inside the main doors. The reason this is an ideal place is that it's easy to find, it's very public, and there are always security staff present in these places, especially in the doorways. That gives you peace of mind, and it ensures that the sale will go ahead safely. You can then go off and do your shopping with the extra cash!

Despite the safety concerns which have to be addressed, reselling on Craigslist is a fantastic way to make extra cash, and build a business which you enjoy. The more time you dedicate to your business, the more it will grow, and the faster too. Having said that, remember that this is also meant to be a side business which doesn't encroach completely on your time. Keep your time planning and management in hand and you'll have the best of both worlds.

Bonus Chapter – Interview with Albert in Vancouver, BC, Canada.

Full time reseller on Craigslist

How did you start your reselling business? And why?

Well, I didn't start reselling computer hardwares right away, I first started just selling stuff at home, like old cellphone, clothes, and just random stuff. The more I sell, the more I take it seriously, because you realized there are so many people browsing on Craigslist, everyone is different, but most people just want to get rid of the stuff they no longer need, so they price their item really low.

What do you find the hardest when selling on Craigslist?

Sometimes it is my English, because English is not my first language, so sometimes I misunderstand people, but most of the time, my English is enough for Reselling on Craigslist.

How much do you make a month for reselling?

To be very honest, from 1200-2500 if you are talking about just profit. On Monday to Thursday, there are less people browsing, but for Friday and Saturday, it can be crazy.

Do you think everyone can make money on craigslist?

Yes and No, and depending on what you are selling and where your location is. In Vancouver, there's quite a lot of people, so there are more money to be made. If you are in a small town, chances are there are much less people buying and selling.

How much time do you spend a day for the business?

Around 6-10, it depends sometimes. When I am not able to find any good deals, then I'll just skip a day and do something else, like listing or renew listings.

Do you people always pay what you ask for?

NO, people always want a lower price. Sometimes, for example you are listing something for 500, they will ask for 250?? You can pretty much expect different kinds of people buying your stuff. However, some people will just pay without negotiating at all. It all just depends on luck and timing. Don't get offended if people are lowballing you. You can just reply nicely saying no or give them another offer.

What is the most fun or enjoyable task when you are doing reselling?

I enjoy browsing on craigslist and just looking a deal , I can browse for 1-2 straight sometimes and it's fun when you are able to find a good deal. However, you need to be careful when something is too cheap. There might be problem with the item. It's always a good idea to check the item you buy in case of scam.

Why do you sell computer or computer hardwares?

Well, because I know how to build a computer and I know quite a lot in terms of how much a computer hardware worth. I do it 2 ways. Sometimes I will buy a computer and take everything out and sell it separately, but sometimes I buy different hardwares and put them all together and sell them as a whole PC.

What do you recommend doing if someone wants to sell computer and computer hardwares?

First, you need to know the price of all hardwares, you need to know how to put a PC together as well as how to separate the parts. I highly recommend learning from youtube videos, because nowadays, there are so many free video you can learn from. You also need to know the performance of the hardwares, especially CPUs and Video cards.

How many kinds of CPUs or Video cards there are?

1000ssss.. sometimes I don't know exactly how well a cpu or video card performs, I have to check on the internet.

What else do you think its profitable for reselling?

Books, video games and toys

What exactly do you do in your business?

A lot of different thing. I post new listing, browse for deals, negotiating with people, taking photo of items I list (good quality photo) and driving out to meet up.

What is the most important task when doing reselling?

Listing your ads correctly is the most important, because you can't price it too high or too low, your photo has to be clear, your ads has to be as professional as it can be, so people will trust you. People are skeptical, because they know they are buying used item, so be friendly and nice to build up trust.

Do you have some tips for people who just got started?

Yes, you need to know and understand the market for the item you are selling . Focus on a set of item, for example, maybe book. Then just sell books. Also, everyone should just start selling thing you no longer need, so you can just learn the process of reselling with no risk. Remember don't invite people to your home if possible. Always meet up at public place with a lot of people.

How much can you expect to make from each sale?

If I bought something for 100, I will need the item to sell for at least 130 to be profitable, because you have to list, meet up and resell, so it won't be worth it if I can't make at least 30% profit.

What is the most profitable item you sold?

A gaming pc, I remember buying a desktop PC for around 200$. I added a video card to make it into a gaming PC. I think I got 470$ profit from that flip. Just one flip. But of course, it's not easy to find this kind of deal. I would make around 150-250 problem selling gaming pcs.

Did you ever experience scam when buying from other people?

Most people are honest, I would say 95%. But Yes, I once bought a PC from someone, there are a lot of problem on that pc, the power button is not work, power supply has some problem and the ethernet card has some problem as well. At that time. I was just focusing on the spec of the PC and didn't check everything, so it's important to check before you buy.

Is driving important for reselling?

If you are doing reselling full time, yes. If not, you can sometimes ask the person to meet places close to you, but in many cases, people won't deliver for free

Last question, what are the advantage of reselling vs a traditional 9-5 job?

This really depends, and your personality, because when you have a job, it's stable and you get a paycheck every 2 weeks or a month, depending on where you live, but if you are doing reselling, income is not as stable. The good thing about reselling is that you can control your own time and not stuck at one place (eg in a warehouse or in an office). You get to meet different people and driving to different place.

For me, Reselling is a much more enjoyable comparing to a 9-5 job. That's for sure. I also enjoy building computer, so that is a win win.

The best thing to do is asking " Are you happy doing what you are doing? " If not, do something else and don't get trapped by your job just because you need the paycheck. Life is way too short.

The Secret Routine of a Craigslist Power-Reseller

The Winning Actionable Tactics to Win on Craigslist

Steve Johnson

Table of Contents

Introduction
    What This Book is About
    What Does it Take to be a Top Craigslist Seller?

Chapter 1: The Importance of a Winning Routine
    Why is a Routine Important Generally?
    How to Organize Your Craigslist Reselling Routine Effectively
    Main Points From This Chapter

Chapter 2: Having Fun is The Most Important Thing
    Do Not Allow Reselling to Become a Burden on Your Time
    The Best Mindset For a Craigslist Reseller
    Main Points From This Chapter

Chapter 3: Patience is Key
    Can't Read My Poker Face
    Main Points From This Chapter

Chapter 4: Hedge Your Bets With Several Listings
    Knowing When to Renew Your Listings
    Have a General Meet up Time
    Main Points From This Chapter

Chapter 5: The Right Way to Negotiate
    Setting Your Price
    Expect And Accept The Lowball Attempt
    Main Points From This Chapter

Chapter 6: Where to Find Quality Items to Resell
    What Makes a Good Item, And What Makes a Bad Item?
    Main Points From This Chapter

Conclusion

Introduction

These days there are more ways to make money than you might originally realize. Passive income allows us to create a new line of income at the side of our regular job, without much effort. Of course, we all live busy lives, so this is ideal!

If you haven't heard of Craigslist, it's time to get with the program! Of course, the chances are that you are certainly very au fait with Craigslist by picking up this book, an advanced guide on how to resell items during the famous website, and therefore earn yourself a nice little sideline. We advise you to read the previous two books in this series, to give you a thorough overview of what Craigslist can do for you, and how to earn cash by reselling items. After that, this book will arm you with all the hints, tips, and knowledge you need to not only resell to success but make a great profit out of it in the process.

It is entirely possible to make a minimum of a part-time salary equivalent by selling items on Craigslist, but there is a huge potential to make more. Countless sellers go on to make a full-time salary every single month, and they do this by putting in as little time as possible. Can you imagine an extra full-time salary on top of your regular earnings? You'll certainly be able to afford some of the finer things in life or save up enough cash for something special.

Reselling via Craigslist gives you the freedom and opportunity to earn cash and have fun at the same time; that's the first thing you should focus on in fact - fun!

We should mention that reselling on Craigslist is probably not going to bring you great gains if you live in a small town or village. In order to make a profit you need to cast your net wide, and although Craigslist is a site for selling locally, it's better to do it all in a large town or city! It really doesn't take a rocket scientist to figure out that the more people you can reach, the higher your potential for sales and profits.

What This Book is About

This book is going to give you all the hints and tips you need to know in order to make a major success of your adventure into Craigslist reselling. The advanced tactics we're going to cover are proven and come from some of the best full-time sellers on Craigslist itself. These people make a full-time salary every single month without fail, and they know exactly what they're talking about! Being kind souls, they've given us access to their tips for success, and from there you can emulate their profits for yourself. Of course, there is a good dose of luck involved in any sideline business, but it is hard to fail at something when you put in the time, the effort, and you take advice from those who know what they are doing.

What we're not going to cover is the basics of actually how to resell on Craigslist, we're going to assume you already know that as you have picked up a book on advanced techniques! As before however, we recommend you read our first two books in this series, to give you all the information you need. From there, you will have a full overview of what you are getting yourself into, and how it might sit in your current lifestyle. The chances are that reselling items on Craigslist will turn into a fun sideline venture for you, and something which actually ends up being a hobby above all else.

What Does it Take to be a Top Craigslist Seller?

So, before we move onto our first actionable chapter, exactly what does it take to be a top reseller on Craigslist? What traits and skills do you need to have?

Here are just a few ideas.

- Determination

- Patience
- An interest in reselling
- A desire to find a hobby you enjoy
- A little space and time
- An eye for a bargain
- Resilience

At the end of the day, reselling on Craigslist should be a fun way to make a little extra cash. If you find that your selling endeavors are starting to be a drain on your time, you need to reassess how you're going about it, and whether you want to continue. If however, you can keep it light and fun, this is going to be a fantastic way to line your bank account.

So, without further ado, let's begin and move onto our first chapter of advanced selling techniques, giving you the mindset and lowdown on how to make a major success of your reselling passive income method.

Chapter 1 - The Importance of a Winning Routine

For this first chapter, we're going to assume that you either have a job already, either full time or part time or that you have other responsibilities, e.g. you have a family which you look after. Reselling on Craigslist is, therefore, a sideline, a method of passive income which doesn't take up much of your time, but brings profits. Of course, just because it doesn't take up a huge amount of time doesn't mean you shouldn't be organized and have a routine. If you want to do well, you need to have the right mindset from the get-go.

In order to succeed at anything in life, a routine is vital. This doesn't even have to be about reselling, this point is about generally winning at life. Being unorganized and not having a routine breeds a stressful situation, and no good can ever come of that. If you're organized and if you have a routine which allows you to do all the things within a day that you need to do, you'll be less stressed, and you'll effectively create more hours in a day (virtually speaking).

When you're trying to earn extra cash by reselling on Craigslist one of the best pieces of advice is to ensure that you have a routine in general, and you also have a routine in terms of how you go about your reselling endeavors. This will become second nature after a while, just as any routine in life does.

Why is a Routine Important Generally?

A routine in life helps you to look after yourself properly. A routine keeps you fit and healthy, and it is good for your mental health too. For instance, you have a routine when you wake up until you go to bed. You wake up at around the same time every day, thanks to your alarm clock. You get up, you brush your teeth, you have a wash, you get dressed, do your hair, and you have breakfast. From there, you go to work, you do the jobs you need to do throughout the day, you come home, have dinner, chill out, and then you go to bed.

A routine isn't boring, a routine ensures order in life. It ensures that you meet your nutritional requirements, it ensures you get enough sleep, and it keeps you healthy in mind and body. A chaotic life which doesn't have any type of routine is the fast track to forgetting things, losing opportunities, and basically creating a chaotic future too. By implement some kind of rough routine at the very least, you're avoiding such issues and actually bringing more opportunities your way.

Most of us have a routine at work too, to ensure that certain important jobs which need to be done daily are actually done on time and to a high quality. For instance, maybe when you arrive in the office you check your emails and reply to those which need it, you then create your to-do list and prioritize it in order, open the incoming mail, and set about your tasks. At the end of the day, perhaps you do a certain task, e.g. the outgoing mail. Routines ensure order, and they're necessary for a life of far less stress.

Ironically, when you have a regular routine in your life, e.g. you go to bed at the same time, you exercise on a regular basis, you spend time with the ones you love, and you go to work on set days of the week, this indirectly helps you to perform better at the other things in your life, e.g. your Craigslist reselling side-line, because you're well rested and content.

How to Organize Your Craigslist Reselling Routine Effectively

The same routine mindset goes when talking about your Craigslist reselling. You need to have a routine which you go through, which helps you to ensure every step of the journey is traveled. From your initial listing stage, you need to go through the procedure of regularly answering queries and speaking to potential buyers. Once a sale is confirmed, you need to arrange a meetup, go to the meetup, exchange the product for the cash, etc.

It's a good idea to have a set time when you deal with a set task. For instance, between 7-8pm at night you do your listings. This will then become your Craigslist listing time and you won't forget to do it. Nothing can become a drain on your time when it is part of your regular routine. You could also have a set time when you regularly meet up with buyers, although this may be more difficult to set if you have some who work odd shifts. A general time slot, however, will be enough to fit into your routine.

You could also have set days which you dedicate a portion of time to your reselling, and the rest of the time you simply answer messages and don't give a huge amount of your day towards it. However you want to arrange it, but your Craigslist reselling should become part of your routine. As with your work to do list, you should also prioritize any tasks you have relating to your reselling and work through them in order of importance.

Never underestimate the power and importance of a routine in any aspect of your life!

Main Points From This Chapter

Let's sum up the main points from this chapter, to give you a quick snapshot of what we have learned. In this section we have talked about the most basic advanced technique there is - having a routine and looking after yourself. Indirectly, this helps with your Craigslist reselling.

- Having a routine helps create order in your life and stops everything becoming chaotic
- Making sure you get enough sleep, you're eating correctly, etc, will indirectly benefit your Craigslist reselling efforts

- You should also have a routine in terms of how you actually do your reselling, e.g. a set time of the week or day when you reply to messages, do meetups, and do your listings
- Reselling should not impact on your life to the point where it becomes a burden, and should slot easily into your regular life, and not create a huge problem overall.

Chapter 2: Having Fun is The Most Important Thing

Whilst you're probably getting into reselling because you want to earn some cash, you should also enjoy it! If you don't have some fun and enjoy the whole process, perhaps getting a buzz of excitement when you find a bargain to resell, or when you actually sell an item, then what's the point? If it's just about making cash with zero enjoyment, you might as well not bother, it's not an actual job after all!

The truth of the matter is that reselling isn't going to be for everyone. Nothing in life is, and one size never fits all. Whilst a huge number of people enjoy reselling and make a good amount of cash from it, not everyone does, and not everyone likes meeting people and selling goods. If it's not for you, it's no big deal, but you won't know that until you try for yourself.

A good idea is to try reselling on a part-time basis and see how you feel about it. Does it fit in well around the rest of your daily commitments? Can you free up just a little time? Do you actually find it fun? Are you making money? Ask yourself those questions after a few sales and assess whether or not to continue from there. It's never a good idea to simply pass an idea off because you think it won't work. How do you know? You might be passing up on a fantastic money earning, a fun-filled hobby if you don't at least give it a good go.

Much of whether or not you enjoy reselling on Craigslist will come down to attitude. If you go into it with a negative mindset and don't expect much from it, you'll never really enjoy it. On the other hand, if you go into it with a realistic, but hopeful mindset, the possibilities are endless.

You will enjoy reselling on Craigslist if you like the following things:

- Shopping - You need to find items to resell and that means doing some bargain hunting
- Finding a bargain - Again, if you get a thrill out of a real deal, you'll love this part of the reselling process
- Creative writing - You need to write listings which grab the attention, and those who love writing will enjoy this part of it
- Talking to new people - You'll have to communicate either on the phone or via email in the original stages of a sale, and if you enjoy talking to new people, this is a good indicator of reselling enjoyment
- The thrill of making a sale - Who doesn't love this part?
- Meeting new people in person - When you hand over the goods and receive the cash, you'll get to meet new people, and you'll probably get to have a chat at the same time

That's really the process broken down into the positive parts. You don't have to make reselling complicated, it can be as simple as the list above.

Do Not Allow Reselling to Become a Burden on Your Time

If you allow reselling to become a drain or burden on your time, it's not going to be enjoyable, it's really that simple. Whether or not you make money, fun is the most important part. You can only do well in life at absolutely anything if you really enjoy it on some level.

For instance, if you go to work every day to earn cash, it's quite likely that there are many parts of your job you really don't like, but there are bound to be some parts which you do enjoy too. If you didn't, you'd have moved on to another job by now, right?

Keep fun at the forefront of your mind and you'll have a greater shot at Craigslist reselling success. Just ask any of the full-time wage-earning Craigslist resellers, and they'll tell you the same thing!

The Best Mindset For a Craigslist Reseller

We know that reselling on Craigslist should be a fun endeavor that brings you cash, and we have talked about the traits of a good Craigslist reseller, but what is the best mindset to have? How do you actually need to think?

Our first chapter highlighted the importance of a routine, and that means that you need to approach reselling as part of your life, but rather than placing it in the work category, it should be in the free-time/hobby category. This will ensure that it remains fun, and not a burden. It's also important not to expect too much, but also not to expect too little.

When you first begin reselling, you'll probably do it the first time as something you don't expect much from. That's fine; Craigslist reselling isn't for everyone, but if you go through it with the right idea and the right mindset, you're more likely to get great results. The best way to think is to be sure you're going to make a profit. That gives you a positive mindset from the get-go. What you shouldn't do is get too ahead of yourself. Do not expect to become a millionaire from reselling, but do expect to make extra cash that will come in very handy indeed. Basically, expect something, but don't expect everything.

To sum up, the winning mindset for a Craigslist reseller is:

- Know that you will make a sale but don't put a time limit on it, it could take weeks
- Understand that you're going to meet people who may not want to pay the price you're asking and that it's perfectly fine to walk away if you feel they aren't going to reach a suitable piece of middle ground with you
- Always deal with people in a respectful and friendly way, regardless of the situation

- It's okay to walk away from a sale that you really feel isn't going anywhere, and there will always be another buyer at some point
- Know that you will make a profit, but do not put a target figure on it
- To expect results, but do not expect miracles
- To allow reselling to be a fun endeavor that enriches your life and becomes an enjoyable hobby, not a job which saps your energy

Main Points From This Chapter

This chapter has covered the winning mindset you need to adapt to be a quality reseller on Craigslist, but it has also talked about the fact that fun is everything in this regard. You cannot and should not allow your reselling to become a burden on your time, and to become something you do not enjoy, or even dread doing. Remember, reselling won't be for everyone, but should give it a try to at least find out.

- Expect to make a profit and expect to have positive outcomes, but don't expect miracles
- Craigslist reselling will not be for everyone, but you should try it at the very least, otherwise, you will never know
- Highlight the areas of reselling that you enjoy, e.g. sourcing out bargains, meeting people, writing creative listing descriptions, and really focus your time on that part
- Nothing in life is worth doing unless you enjoy it, and the same goes for Craigslist reselling
- You will earn cash from reselling, and that should be an important reason to try it, but it should not be the single most important reason.

Chapter 3: Patience is Key

If you think the moment you start reselling on Craigslist you're going to instantly find yourself raking in the cash and having sales left, right, and center, you might be quite mistaken. Patience is one of the most important traits of a successful Craigslist reseller, and you need to be able to make complete peace with the fact that you may not sell your products quickly, or sometimes at all.

It's not unusual for a sale to sometimes take weeks or even months to be completed. In some cases, it will never sell and you might have to tweak a few details. There are a few lessons to be learned here, however, but patience is the key point you need to remember at all times.

Don't Become Disappointed if Nobody Contacts You Quickly

As we've just mentioned, it's not unusual for sales to take a while. This isn't like eBay, which is a huge international site. You are only advertising to those within your local area, and that isn't the same catchment as national or international! This basically means it could take a little longer, and that's something you should just be aware of and be okay with.

Don't be Tempted to Lower Your Item Drastically Because it Hasn't Sold Yet

The other key point to remember is that you shouldn't be tempted to lower the price of your item by a huge amount, simply because it hasn't sold yet. You could tweak it a little and reduce it slightly, but you shouldn't drastically drop it, in order to get people to sit up and take notice. A slight alteration is enough to make your listing more noticeable again, refreshing it in many ways, and that could be enough to grab someone's attention and make a sale.

Always be Friendly And Patient When Taking to People

There are always going to be times when you're speaking to someone and you think they're interested, but they suddenly go cold on you and act indifferent. That's normal and that is also part of human nature. Don't allow that situation to make you less patient, or less friendly with people contacting you about sales. Just because they don't seem to want to buy your item, isn't a reason to be rude.

In some cases, they may change their mind. Of course, if you were rude or you lacked patience, they're probably not going to come back to you, and you've lost a sale. On the other hand, if you remain patient and friendly, they may think twice and end up buying your item in the end. Friendliness doesn't cost a thing.

We're going to talk a little later on about a few ways to maximize your sales, but listing your items at the right time is one of them. In this case, we're not talking about a specific time of day, but a specific time of year. For instance, if you have an item which is seasonal, there is no point in listing it at a time which isn't going to grab attention. If on the other hand, you bide your time, there is more chance of a sale.

For example, perhaps you have some second hand Playstation games to resell. These would sell quite well at any time of year, but if you wait until around November time, you might find more interest, because Christmas is around the corner. The same school of thought could be adopted for trying to resell a lawnmower. This might be a useful piece of kit at any time of year, but it is more likely to sell during the spring and summer months.

Can't Read My Poker Face

Reselling items on Craigslist is like playing poker in so many ways. You should not let on to a potential buyer that you are keen to sell. An air of indifference is something you need to develop.

Of course, you can still be indifferent whilst maintain a polite, kind, and patient demeanor, but you need to practice that poker face! An experienced buyer will be able to smell your desperation to sell quite a long way off. As a result, they will assume that because you want to sell so badly, you're likely to accept far lower as a final price. Even if you don't accept a price that is drastically lower, they will know that you are more likely to accept less than you've asked for. This means you're going to lose money, and that's not what this whole game is about! It's also probably going to make you feel less euphoric about making a sale, and there's no fun in that either.

Some very experienced buyers will also attempt to cut the price to see what your reaction is. Again, a poker face is what you need. They may even walk away from the sale, just to see how you react. Poker face once more! In many cases, they will come back and simply buy the item for what you have asked, and if they don't, it doesn't matter; there will always be another buyer.

Get practicing that poker face in the mirror before you start with your reselling efforts!

Main Points From This Chapter

If you're not a naturally patient person, you need to attempt to adopt this very mindset. Successful Craigslist reselling requires patience. It's very possible that you will list an item and it will not sell for weeks, possibly even months, and you need to be prepared for this, and okay with it. Don't allow yourself to lose your patience with people you deal with, and don't show any kind of emotion in terms of how badly you want to make a sale.

- You need to be patient with sales - it may take weeks, it might even take months. Have faith!
- Always treat every person you speak to with regards to your reselling with patience and kindness. Creating a good first impression is vital and that sometimes means biting your tongue when you meet someone who is less than friendly back to you - always be the bigger person!
- You also need to develop what is known as your poker face. Never allow your face to give you away, e.g. if you are quite keen to sell something. The buyer will sense it and try and cut your price down to a level you are not willing to sell
- Don't be tempted to lower your price drastically just because you haven't made a sale - it's not worth simply making a sale for the hell of it if you're not making a profit.

Chapter 4: Hedge Your Bets With Several Listings

If you have read our earlier books on this subject you will know that we didn't recommend you have more than one or two listings active at one time whilst you familiarized yourself with selling on Craigslist. That is a truth, but once you've made one or two sales, it's time to become more advanced and start hedging your bets. Once you're familiar, it's all systems go!

Another advanced selling technique from some of the best in the business is to have several listings active at one time. This means you need to be organized, and that calls back to our earlier point of having a routine. If you can do that, you'll easily be able to juggle the tasks related to the selling procedure, without missing something or causing a delay.

It doesn't take a genius to figure that the more listings you have, the more chances there are of a customer reaching out and potentially purchasing one of your items. The more you spread your net, the more purchasing options there will be, and sales are far more likely as a result.

Work out how many listings is comfortable for you and work with it. You can always tweak it at a later date and add more, or pull back if you think you might have gone too far the last time. Remember, this is supposed to be your side hustle, your passive income method which doesn't take up a huge amount of your time. If you notice that you have too many listings and it's all becoming somewhat of a burden, you need to think more carefully about how many listings you place next time. Learn from your experiences.

Equally, you might find that you have time to place a few more listings and in that case, go for it!

It's a good idea to write down your listings as you create them and whenever progress is made on one of them, e.g.

someone contacts you and asks to meet up to purchase the item, write that down too. You will then know where you are with each sale, and you won't get confused and potentially take the wrong item to the wrong buyer! That would be a huge issue which would cost you time and potentially a sale.

Knowing When to Renew Your Listings

Another advanced technique you need to think carefully about is when to renew your listings.

As we mentioned in our previous chapter, you need to be patient when reselling on Craigslist, and it might not happen overnight; it's more likely to happen in weeks than it is days actually. In that case, you might feel the need to renew your listing, effectively refreshing it and taking it to the top of the interest pile. Your renowned listing will then be within the 'most recent' category, and we all know that most people browse those first, before digging deeper into specific categories. By doing this, you're catching the general browsing public, and not only those who want to purchase a specific item, within that specific category.

There are some good times to renew listings and some not so great times. For instance, if you renew an item in the middle of the night, most people are sleeping and therefore not going to see it when it is first renewed. Remember, you're dealing with a local selling site here, not a national one, and most people within your local area are probably asleep, getting ready for work the next day! Avoid late nights and very early mornings for listings and instead, look towards the 8 pm to 11 pm window.

This is a good time because during this space, most people have finished dinner, and they're sat browsing on their devices, passing the time and relaxing. These are prime Internet shopping times in general, so you should take advantage of that fact. By renewing your listing when people are more likely to be idly browsing Craigslist, you raise your chances of making a sale dramatically.

During the day, most people are busy with work and their other commitments, but if you stick to early evenings, you'll probably find greater success with your selling efforts.

Have a General Meet up Time

We talked earlier about having a routine, and part of that routine should be a general meet up time window you have. Of course, this could change occasionally depending upon who you sell your items to, and you do need to be a little adaptive if you want to make sales. Having said that, having a specific window when you carry out your meets up and swap your items for the cash means that you can create that routine we talked about earlier. You can tweak this for those customers who have unsociable working hours, e.g. they can only meet up in the mornings or during lunch breaks, but these occasions are probably going to be few and far between.

Overall, most people who buy items from Craigslist arrange to meet up for collection after they have finished work. Of course, this time can vary, but generally speaking, that is around 5 pm to 7 pm overall. If you can have a general meet up time like that, you'll find that most of your meets up fit into this and you can minimize the amount of impact Craigslist reselling has on the rest of your free time.

Main Points From This Chapter

In this chapter, we've talked about the advanced technique of having several listings on the go at any one time. It's important to do so if you want to increase your chances of making a sale. When you first start to try reselling, it's a good idea to stick with just one or two, of course, until you familiarize yourself, but once you have made a sale and you know how it works, you can have more than one on the go. This is to be recommended!

- Once you have familiarized yourself with one or two sales and the whole route to take, spread your net wider and have several listings at one time
- Keep a record of your listings and the progress you have made, so you don't become confused between items
- Know the best times to refresh your listings, and avoid obscure times, like in the middle of the night, late at night, early in the mornings, etc. 8pm-11pm is a good time to refresh listings, as this is when most people are browsing Craigslist after dinner
- Have a set time when you meet people, but be flexible if you need to be. Not everyone finishes work at the 'regular' time, and after work is when most people meet up to collect items and hand over the money.

Chapter 5: The Right Way to Negotiate

There's a lot to talk about when it comes to negotiation, and this is certainly the make or break area when it comes to a sale or walking away. The best Craigslist resellers, the ones who make the most cash without it impacting upon their life too much, know how to negotiate professionally.

Remember, you need to be polite, kind, and honest with all your potential buyers. Some of them may not be pleasant people, that's just life, but you need to remain polite at all times to ensure that you do your very best to make the sale happen. Of course, most people are lovely and you'll probably have a sociable side of your Craigslist reselling too. You might meet someone who you stand and talk to for half an hour after you've swapped your item for the cash!

Whoever you meet, and you will meet a lot of them, you should always deal with them in a polite, open, and positive way. Avoid negativity and keep your body language open and positive. Avoid looking away, maintain eye contact, smile, nod, listen to them, don't cross your arms and legs across your body, etc. People can tell when you're being closed off, and it immediately puts them on their guard. In this case, it could mean that a sale doesn't happen. It really can be the smallest things to derail a potential sale.

You should also be aware that some people really love to bargain, in fact, many people purchase items on Craigslist purely for the rush of bargaining and grabbing an item for a lower price. It really is a rush, but from a seller's point of view, you need to be aware of this issue.

So, how should you deal with someone who is bargaining until they're blue in the face? That's where setting your price comes in, and we're going to cover that in a second. For now, however, it's important to be accommodating but only to a certain degree. Know how low you're willing to go and don't go below that. Remember, you're in this to make a profit not to make a loss!

Setting Your Price

We've established that some people love to bargain, but by being clever with your price setting you can give them that thrill that they think they're getting when in actual fact you're still getting the price you wanted all along. Sneaky!

The best-advanced technique to be aware of on price is to always list an item for a little higher than you're actually happy to sell for. Don't go way over the top, as that isn't going to attract buyers in the first place, but just a little. The situation will then go one of two ways.

Firstly, you're contacted by someone who pays you the price you have listed. Great news, you're getting extra profits and they don't even try to lower the price.

Secondly, you're contacted by someone who loves to bargain. This means that they are going to try and lower the price. The thing is, if you only allow them to lower it by a little, e.g. the price you were happy to sell at in the first place, you've not lost anything! Everyone's winner; they think they're getting a bargain and they have their little bartering thrill, and you get the price you wanted all along. That is the best outcome for everyone.

Of course, never let the buyer know that this is your strategy, otherwise, you're completely defeating the object.

The fact that your buyer thinks you've given them a good discount also does a lot for your reputation as a seller. Remember, you need to treat your reselling endeavors as a business, and every business needs to maintain a good reputation. Your buyer is more likely to look out for items you're selling in the future, and therefore choose you over another buyer because they've dealt with you in the past and had a positive experience.

You might want to learn more about how to actually come to the right price in the first place. If you're new to reselling, you might not have the first clue about prices to put onto items, but that is where research will serve you well. Whenever you purchase an item to resell, you'll know what you paid for it, and if you got it for free, you should do some research online to find the most common prices. From there, research more - how much is the item selling for locally? How much do you need to make a profit?

We can't give you a hard and fast figure here, because it really depends on the item you're selling and how popular it is. For instance, a popular item is more likely to sell for a higher price, than an unpopular item. That's just common sense. It's about supply and demand, and opting for products which are more in demand means you can actually ask for higher prices. Research is your friend here, but remember that you're in this for a profit, not for a loss!

Expect And Accept The Lowball Attempt

When someone lowballs you, they are basically trying to get you to sell for a ridiculously low price and they will throw all manner of pleading looks your way. Some people may attempt to pull at your heartstrings, some may be a little more aggressive with their buying endeavors, but however they do it, it's likely that you'll feel the need to lower your price.

Do not do this!

Someone who gets you to lower your price through lowballing tactics knows what they are doing!

Basically, the best piece of advice to give here is to expect that you're going to be lowballed, and just accept it as a part of

Craigslist life. Nothing is 100% positive, and in terms of reselling and making cash on Craigslist, that is about those who will try and get you to cut your prices in deceptive ways.

You have to look at it this way - they're trying to bag a bargain, and you can't fault them for trying, but it's up to you whether you accept it or not. If you want to be taken seriously as a seller and you want to make cash and not make losses then you need to refuse lowballing attempts in the most polite and friendly way you can and walk away.

Don't become offended when someone tries to lowball you, you can easily just politely tell them that you can't lower your price to that level and give them the lowest you're happy to go to, or you can ignore their messages after you have initially said no. If they continue to message you, again, ignore.

Some buyers can be quite aggressive in their lowballing attempts, but it's up to you whether or not you rise to it. The best advice is to not even respond and simply wait for the right buyer to come your way. Never be afraid to say no if the situation isn't right - any buyer isn't the right buyer, the right buyer will purchase your item, or items, for the right price for you. Sometimes walking away isn't a mistake.

Main Points From This Chapter

This chapter has been about how to negotiate in the best way, and we've shared some hints and tips from some of the best Craigslist resellers in the business. The art of negotiation is one you need to traverse carefully, as otherwise, you're likely to end up with far less than your item is worth. Remember, the whole point of Craigslist is to make a profit and if you're constantly making a loss because your negotiating skills need improvement, there is no point at all!

- Realize that there are some people who love to find bargains, and as such, they use this has their hobby

- Do some research and find out how much you should ask for, e.g. to set the appropriate price and not go under what it is worth
- Set your price a little higher than you originally would like, and that way your seller will feel like you're giving them a discount, therefore satisfying their bargain hunting side, but in actual fact, you're still selling for the price you wanted
- Understand that lowballing attempts are just part and parcel of the process, and don't become annoyed or aggrieved when someone tries to cut the price down to a ridiculously low amount
- If you feel you are not going to get the price you want, don't be afraid to walk away from the sale, in a polite manner, and know that another buyer will come at another time.

Chapter 6: Where to Find Quality Items to Resell

It's all very well and good talking about how to sell items on Craigslist and what not to do, but where do you find those items from in the first place?

Success starts at the very first point and that means sourcing out the lowest priced items, that you can sell for higher prices through your listings. Some of this takes work, but once you get a little more used to reselling, you'll find items far quicker as a result.

There are several places you can find quality reselling items:

- **On Craigslist's Free Section** - If you regularly check Craigslist's free section, you'll usually find some great, quality items that you can then resell on for a price. This means you're getting the greatest profit because the item never cost you anything in the first place. Of course, you should be careful which items you source from here, as you should only go for the quality. Once more - reputation is everything when it comes to becoming a quality seller.
- **On Craigslist in General** - You can find bargains on Craigslist by browsing carefully and selecting items at low prices to sell on for higher profits. This is going to take a little time, but again, it is something you'll get used to the more you do it. With experience, you'll quickly be able to recognize bargains.
- **In Charity/Thrift Shops** - Whilst you're out shopping, why not call into the local charity shop and look for a few bargains. This way you're doing a good deed by helping out the local charity, but you're also finding some great items to resell on Craigslist. Secondhand markets are also a good place to look, including flea markets and car boot sales. It's really a case of always being on the lookout for a good bargain to sell on for a higher price.

- **On eBay** - eBay has long been a good place to look for bargains and if you manage to find something which is very low in price and can be resold, go ahead and purchase it! Don't spend too much time searching, but if you're browsing during your lunch hour, you could find a few items.
- **On Social Media Selling Sites** - Social media often has selling pages or even gifting pages, where you can find low cost, or sometimes free, items to resell on. Again, it's about being aware of these and looking on occasion, but not dedicating a huge amount of time. Remember, this is supposed to be a fun thing, not something which becomes a full-time job, or a drain on your time.
- **Via a Clear Out in Your Own Home** - Regular decluttering sessions can often yield some fantastic items to sell on for a profit, and they're free because you already own them! Make it a routine that once every so often you have a declutter and get rid of anything which you really don't need or use.

These are some of the best places to source items which you can resell on Craigslist, and many of them are extremely low cost or even free. Simply keep your eyes open when you're out and about and always have 'bargains' on your mind!

What Makes a Good Item, And What Makes a Bad Item?

What should you look for in a reselling item, and what should you avoid?

Firstly, you need to have a niche area, to avoid getting confused. If you have a niche, you are sure of your prices, and you can answer questions confidently and carefully from your buyers. Buying absolutely anything is not going to give you a look of professionalism. For that reason, most successful Craigslist resellers specialize in a certain area, e.g. computer hardware, automobile accessories, etc. By doing this, you build up a good reputation, and customers react very positively to that.

The features of a good item are:

- In perfect working order
- No visible signs of wear and tear, and if so they are very minimal
- A product which is in demand in your area
- Low priced
- Confident that you can sell on for a profit
- Preferably in the box, with all accessories included
- A big brand name, e.g. an Apple product will always sell well

The features of a bad item are:

- Any signs of breakage, or moderate to severe wear and tear
- A product which is quite obscure, e.g. not that in demand
- Missing important accessories, e.g. a charger
- High in price to purchase in the first place, therefore making it hard to score a profit
- Old or outdated
- A brand name that nobody has heard of

As you can see, finding good versus bad products isn't really that difficult, it's simply a case of knowing that certain products will always sell better than others. That is something you will learn as you become more experienced in your reselling efforts.

Basically, ask yourself this question - 'will this product sell?' That's really all you need to know.

Main Points From This Chapter

This chapter has talked about where to source items to resell on Craigslist, and what exactly makes a good product versus a bad one. There are many places you can find items to resell, and it's really about being aware and always have your eyes out for a bargain.

- You will find good items to resell on Craigslist whilst you're out and about doing your regular shopping etc, and you need to simply always be aware of possible bargains to resell on
- Don't forget that your own home is a good place to find items too - most of us don't realize how much we have in our homes which we don't use, and this can be sold on for a profit
- Some of the best places include free Craigslist sections, general Craigslist sections, other auction sites, such as eBay, social media selling pages, e.g. Facebook, and from decluttering your own home. You could even look in charity shops, thrift stores, on flea markets, and at car boot sales
- Do not spend too much time sourcing out items, remember this is supposed to be a sideline, not a full-time job
- Understand the things which make a good item, e.g. no breaks, no signs of wear and tear, accessories and box if necessary
- Also understand the thing which makes a poor item, e.g. breaks, an old model, poor quality.

Conclusion

And there we have it! You now know all the insider advanced tips on how to become a top quality Craigslist reseller. You have all the information you could need to not only sell items for a profit but enjoy it and make a real sideline business out of it too.

This book is designed to show you the potential that Craigslist reselling has in terms of making cash. This isn't something you will only possibly make money from - if you put in the time and effort, the rewards certainly will come. With that in mind, however, Craigslist reselling is not for everyone. If you live in a small town or village, you're not going to have the right number of possible buyers to make a real go of your efforts. If however, you live in a large town or city, you have a range of people you can reach out to, and you're sure to meet some real characters as a result! Some of these people you will not connect with at all, but others could turn out to be friends you end up socializing with in the future. You really never know until you give it a try.

The great thing about trying reselling is that you're not actually taking any undue risks. You're not really spending money in order to see if it works. Try it out with something you already have as the first listing, e.g. something you have in your house that you think will see. See where you go from there. If you like it, carry on with it. If you don't, at least you tried and now you know.

As we've mentioned a few times already, we have two other books in this series which give you the basics of Craigslist reselling, but this book is designed to give you the advanced side of things. By reading this book, you are arming yourself with the knowledge and know-how on how to master reselling and make a good profit out of it. When you first look at the whole idea of reselling items for cash, you'll probably think there really isn't too much cash to be made, but it's actually not the case. Provided you dedicate the right attitude towards it, and you find a product niche which is in demand and sells well, you'll find the profit potential is quite high.

Craigslist reselling is like anything in life - you get out of it what you put in. Whilst you shouldn't dedicate too much time to your reselling efforts, because it is supposed to be a fun sideline, you should certainly take it just as seriously as any other business endeavor. If you can do that, and if you can use it as a fun part of your routine too, the sky really will be the limit.

Thank you for reading " The Smart Craigslist Collection: 3 Books in 1 Volume ".

*If you enjoyed this book and found this book helpful, please consider leaving a review, **even if it's only a few lines; it would make all the difference and would be very much appreciated. Thank you!***

Steve Johnson

www.ingramcontent.com/pod-product-compliance
Lightning Source LLC
Chambersburg PA
CBHW021832170526
45157CB00007B/2777